UNDER THE BRIDGE
& OVER THE MOON

Kevin Ireland was born in Mt Albert, Auckland, but his family moved across the harbour to Devonport in 1938. In that seaside village, after what seems like a lifetime of further shifts around the world, he now lives and works as a fulltime writer.

UNDER THE BRIDGE & OVER THE MOON

A MEMOIR

Kevin Ireland

V
VINTAGE

Vintage New Zealand
(An imprint of the Random House Group)

18 Poland Road
Glenfield
Auckland 10
NEW ZEALAND

Sydney   New York   Toronto
London   Auckland   Johannesburg
and agencies throughout the world

First published 1998

© Kevin Ireland 1998
The moral rights of the Author have been asserted.

Printed in Malaysia
ISBN 1 86941 363 6

CONTENTS

FOREWORD

A memoir should be a bit like a conversation over a drink — the talk should be intimate yet deceptive. It should have shape, yet appear to accumulate, almost accidentally, by digression.

Perhaps not everything that should be recorded here gets the recognition it deserves, but this is not a history book. It is an attempt at a selection of events that gives all the memorable characters at least a chair at the table, even if one or two of those chairs have broken legs.

My sisters and brother would wish to add detail and to present the story quite differently. Although the result would be no less truthful, to invite them to do so would soon have us all spilling the good stuff over the tablecloth.

It seems to me to be very much a question of keeping an eye on the level of the bottle in front of us while glancing occasionally at our wristwatches. That's the way I've always wished to write.

K I

ACKNOWLEDGEMENTS

My profound thanks are due to all the editorial staff at Random House (in particular Juliet Rogers, Harriet Allan and Gillian Kootstra) and to Quentin Wilson of Hazard Press, who published my latest selected poems in *Anzac Day* (1997). Most of the poems that are quoted here can be found in that volume.

Thanks are also due to Michael King (*One of the Boys*, 1988), Michael Gifkins (*Through the Looking Glass*, 1988), Sandra Coney (*Salute to New Zealand*, 1989) and Warwick Roger and Stephen Stratford, editor and deputy editor respectively of the issues of *Metro* that published essays that have found their tangled way from those publications to this.

I should like to acknowledge the use I have been able to make of a family commentary and personal apologia constructed by my mother Clare Ward, and I am most grateful for the useful comments made on an earlier version of this manuscript by my sisters, Ann Fairley and Carole Blair. Any errors of fact or bias that remain must be mine alone — and possibly to an intentional fault.

For Ann Fairley, Carole Blair and Anthony Jowsey,
who were there.

And for Marion Mirko,
who turned up later.

1 : A SHRIMP WITH ATTITUDE

I was born just in time for lunch. My father looked up at the clock and noted in his Masonic Bible that it said exactly ten to twelve. Then he sat down in an armchair and went to sleep. He was exhausted.

My mother had sent him out the previous evening to fetch help because she was certain I was just about to arrive. There was a fog so thick it left glistening beads all over his overcoat, like a heavy sweat, and it was acrid and gritty with the smoke of damped-down winter fires and the coal ranges that most families around Mt Albert still cooked on. The era of the electric stove was yet to come.

My father told me all these details later, as incidents in the living saga that our family celebrated when we gathered around the table or in the sitting-room regularly on Sunday nights for storytelling and readings from books such as *Huckleberry Finn*.

It was a story that had the ring of authenticity. Although my father is now dead, I can close my eyes and still see him describing his part in my arrival. With his hands outstretched, he recites yet again how he had to fumble and bump his way from lamppost to lamppost along Mt Albert Road, where we lived, to find the midwife, and how the street lights were so dim he got lost several times within cooee of his own front door.

The performance was obviously embellished for dramatic effect, but it was made more real by precisely that process. It came to life in the way that fairy stories and other fictions catch the truth through the lustre of their telling. Nothing is less enchanting or less persuasive than a fact told without imagination. We may agree with it, but we won't necessarily *believe* it.

My father would point a finger at me and announce in mock seriousness that the midwife was definitely not pleased to be called out on such a night, and she was even less happy when I decided stubbornly to stay put inside my mother until the sun had almost reached its high point in the grey clouds of winter the following day. He claimed she quite understandably put an extra effort into the slap she gave me when at last I decided to leave the liquid depths of the womb to join the wind-eaters of this world.

So how did my mother feel? She told me that she was too elated at the time to take it all in. Both her brothers had died as babies, and her dearly loved maternal grandmother had had only one child, a girl, so when I was born on the eighteenth of July 1933, she had a chance to succeed where her own mother and grandmother had failed. She already had a healthy, happy daughter in the form of my sister Ann, and now she would raise a male heir.

In those days it was not just a matter of sexual bias to yearn for a boy or two about the home. My mother and her three sisters had spent a large part of their growing-up years on a rough backblocks farm near Whangamomona, in north Taranaki, and experience had taught her that boys could sometimes be useful creatures to breed.

However, as it happened, I would never have been much use in any practical way on a farm. And as for my mother's ambition of reviving a vigorous male line through me, right from the beginning I was of no help to her plans. In spite of the fact that I made an appearance in time for what has since become my favourite meal – a leisurely lunch – I turned out to be what she always described as 'a proper little swine to feed'. There was no way I would eat.

It took a year of the punishing rigours of Karitane nursing to encourage me to learn the first essential for survival, though it now strikes me as even more crazy that I should have disdained the enormous pleasures of the breast as an introduction to the pleasures of the table.

And as if it were not disgrace enough to refuse to eat – in a land of milk and honey, not to mention the kingdom of huge slabs of butter, soggy boiled cabbage and grey mutton stew – the terrible consequence of my intransigence was that through my wilful self-starvation I changed from your average four-kilogram Kiwi baby into a thin and shrivelled runt.

It had nothing to do with owning a mean or miserable disposition, for I was not a bawling or bleating child – indeed, it was my maternal grandfather's proud and probably inaccurate boast that he never heard me once whimper or whinge – I was a born refusenik. Or, at any rate, that's what I like to think, however impossible it is to prove. After all, non-conformity, in its general sense, has proved to be the pattern of my entire life.

Some kids are born with a cussed streak that discipline or cajoling may temporarily suppress, but will never cure. It will always reveal itself through some new gesture of defiance, a sly and dogged commitment to contrariness or a simple bullheaded act of non-compliance. I was one of these subversives. From the word go I was a shrimp with attitude.

And, just in case anyone should assume that I wish to award myself bonus points on this account, let me immediately say that I have never thought there is any special civic or ethical virtue attached to this kind of disposition. At its worst an obstinate contradictoriness ends up in mere self-destruction or crime. And at its most frustrating it offers its victims an excuse to make nuisances of themselves in the name of half-pie theories and cranky causes.

The truly valuable side to non-conformity is that it is as irresistible as the grass that has the power to crack a concrete pathway. It splits the dull neat appearance of our best efforts to crush and conceal the anarchic aspects of our humanity. Yet its reward is seldom more than the private satisfaction of knowing that it can be a privilege to fill your mind with free thought, even at the risk of being in the wrong yet again – though I suppose it's always a consolation to believe you're wrong for the right reasons.

But all that was to come. Unknown to anyone at the time, the winter in which I was born marked just about the bottom of the pit of the Depression. The times were as grim and gloomy for my family as they were for just about everyone else.

The Loan & Mercantile foreclosed the mortgage on my maternal grandfather's farm at Whangamomona and on the other farms that he had bought, or thought he had bought, as his neighbours simply downed tools in despair and walked off their land. He had been a blithe optimist, devoted to fanciful hopes and dreams of landholding grandeur, which would be achieved by unswerving vision and heroic hard work, not to mention a ton or two of gelignite to blast away the huge silver boles of the dead trees and the blackened tombstone stumps that made the central North Island hillsides when I was a boy look like old colonial graveyards.

Yet for all the passion of his commitment, my grandfather left only the faintest trace of his signature across the landscape, for as soon as he was turned off his land and the Loan & Mercantile had padlocked the gate against his re-entry, the farm rapidly reverted to second-growth scrub, gorse and blackberry. The farm buildings soon collapsed, slips blocked the sledge tracks to the back paddocks, and the harrows and discs rusted away in a tangle of weeds.

The 'whare' in which the family lived – with its interior walls coated with a paste made from a mixture of flour, water and alum on which were slapped thick layers of newspapers and pretty pictures cut from calendars and magazines – stood abandoned before the relentless advance of the regenerating bush. Heavy boards had been nailed across every window and door.

To this day the area he farmed is named after him. The McKenney Valley sounds impressive, but it exists only as a name on a local map, and there is now a huge population of possums busily dealing to the bush where there used to be farms and people. As an ironical footnote to the history of the human occupation of our nation, the possum presents a far greater danger to the landscape than my grandfather ever did.

Yet, in spite of all the failure that the 1930s could heap upon the nation, my father and mother could not help being the young and optimistic inheritors of a pioneer tradition which said that, no matter how bad things may seem, they would always pick up again one day. They kept their aspirations high and seemed to have no problem about taking a gamble on the eventual improvement of their prospects.

In 1934 they decided to sell up the little they owned in order to see the world; so at the age of one I went with them to England. My father worked as a steward both ways, in return for a free fare, while my mother travelled with Ann and me in what amounted to steerage class.

It was the first of my many round-the-world trips, but though my sister still remembers a few highlights, the whole experience was entirely wasted on me, except in one important respect. I learned to speak in London.

We lived in Tottenham, near White Hart Lane, where Maurice Gee and I were to travel on Saturday afternoons nearly thirty years later to watch Danny Blanchflower's magical Tottenham Hotspur team (and, as a prime example of how the mind insists on storing useless information, I can still recite the name and position of every player in the side). But in those days the area was associated not just with football – it had become a place of settlement for Jewish immigrants, mainly from Eastern Europe.

UNDER THE BRIDGE & OVER THE MOON

A lot of these excitable and voluble new Londoners spoke Yiddish, and nearly all those who used English did so with a heavy Jewish accent modified by cockney. My first attempted pronouncements from the pram were therefore flavoured with the accents that swirled around it non-stop from morning till night, issuing from our landlady and the constant stream of relatives who dropped in on her, and I couldn't help but sound like an East End Jew.

According to family legend, my first accent was Yiddish, and my father discovered to his bemusement that he was my vader.

2 : MISSION TO MOSCOW

In an odd sort of way, the Depression actually saved me, because it put paid to one of my father's dearest fantasies – one that he may otherwise have made a nightmare reality. The massive and terrible disruption of the world's economy meant no less to me than that it also wrecked my father's ambition that his second child should enjoy the privilege of being born in Moscow, in the Union of Soviet Socialist Republics, rather than in humble Mt Albert, Auckland, New Zealand.

Our trip to England was, for my father, the first stage of a private voyage of homage to Moscow that was as firm in its commitment as any Christian's pilgrimage to Jerusalem or Muslim's haj to Mecca. Nothing would have given him greater pleasure than that a child of his should have been born in the capital of the nation that he believed had witnessed the golden dawn of a new society – the nation that would create the model for paradise on earth. So far as I was concerned, it was a very close shave indeed.

My father actually made it alone to Leningrad, then to Moscow, for a brief Intourist-escorted visit that would inspire him all his life – or, at least, until the lamp of holy truth began to dim in the USSR, later to shine for him again, in all its former glory, in Peking under Mao.

The wonder is that my father never joined the Communist Party, though he may as well have signed up, paid his subs and gone around the streets selling the *People's Voice* or holding up a placard announcing his membership, for he was known as a 'Commie' all around the neighbourhood when I was young.

The thing he always held against the Party was that it was simply pussyfooting around with the problems of the world – it was corrupt with compromise. So far as he was concerned it was not nearly left-wing enough – he wanted worldwide instant action. There was something quite splendidly insane about his politics. He was a Protest Party of one.

How could he have been such a lunatic? I have often thought about it, and the only explanation I can come up with is that he came from a long line of Yorkshire craftsmen who practised staunch and uncompromising Christian Socialist values, and he simply advanced these one stage further into hopeless delusion. Yet, as I once wrote in a poem, I have always been

> impressed by ways or codes . . .
> drawn to irreversible convictions

and I can't help having a totally bowled-over affection for my father's bizarre solo revolutionary zeal and his fortitude in the face of so much well-documented evidence and active hostility against him. He had decided that he was right, he gloried in his sense of personal conviction and there was nothing mean, miserable or concealed about his outlook.

I am at last old enough to know that I have inherited a lot of my own crazy cussedness from him, so it is a consolation for me to believe that when he described himself as a 'progressive' he meant it to be understood that his views on the improvement of society and the betterment of mankind were held for idealistic reasons.

At the very least it means that he was on the side of the angels, even if Joe Stalin most certainly wasn't.

3: TREASURE TROVE

Families are treasure stores of myths that reinforce a sense of belonging to a group of successful survivors. Elizabeth Stone's marvellous book, *Black Sheep and Kissing Cousins: How Our Family*

Stories Shape Us, examines the hidden structures that give importance to our families' definitions, values and rules, and shows the pattern of meaning behind the endless stories of lost fortunes, unheeded warnings, missed opportunities and errant sons and daughters who spurned their families and fell by lonely waysides – always to be balanced by fairy-story accounts of help from unexpected sources, hair's-breadth escapes from disaster, triumphs over adversity and the rewards of mutual support, and by cautionary and sometimes contradictory lessons in the benefits of withstanding temptation while showing cunning in outwitting those who would do you down.

My family was rich in such lore. However, for years the amateur genealogists have been busy on my father's side, so a lot of irritating facts have begun to emerge that are of no interest to those who believe that Elizabeth Stone's perceptions reveal the correct shape of a family's history, and that truth is moulded not from details such as who married whom eight generations back, but from fragile layers of words that gather and gain bonded strength as they are spun from thin air around the dinner table or the fireside, the kind of words that can even end up as poems.

The way I remember it, my father's father was a cabinetmaker called Jowsey and his mother was from a 'footwear' family called Adams. Old man Jowsey was a marvellous artist in wood, from a line of craftsmen whose skills had been handed down from father to son for as far back as family memory could stretch, and included an ancestor who was reckoned to have been a ship's carpenter on one of Nelson's great fleet at the Battle of Trafalgar. They had lived for the past millennium in or near Scarborough and Whitby, in Yorkshire, as many of the family still do to this day. If your name is Jowsey you are certain to be related to this small clan.

A nine-hundred-year-old and possibly quite spurious curiosity from a literary point of view is that Jowsey is said to be a local corruption of Joce, who was one of the Norman warlords (and a descendent of the Viking emigration to northern France) who did his best to lay waste to the northern districts of England and Ireland after Duke William's invasion in 1066. One of Joce's other regional variations is the Irish surname Joyce.

Warriors, Vikings, Norman plunderers, Irish literary gents – it all sounds like a family tree full of romantic interconnections, but the unavoidable reality is that there was merely a bit of pillaging and systematic butchery going on somewhere along the tangled twigs at the end of a twisted branch and a name was acquired somehow or another, and the sap of my forebears carried it out onto a remote bud in a forest of falling leaves.

Who knows *really* how they came by their name? And who should care, so long as it provides a good story? The name may have been picked up in a pub conversation or copied down from a signpost.

My father was born in Scarborough, but when his father, Henry Marflitt Jowsey, was kicked out of his chocolate-box-pink cottage (for disseminating Christian Socialist propaganda) by his employer – who, by another curiosity, was a member of a family that was to supply a future governor-general to Wellington – the Jowseys packed their bags and set sail for a fresh start in a New Zealand, which then had a reputation as the 'social laboratory of the world'.

The names of my father and his brothers provide a neat little window into Edwardian Englishness at the time of their emigration: my father's name was Bernard and his brothers were called Frank, George, Harold and Wilfred (Bill). The sole girl was named Eva.

Henry Marflitt had been forced by his refusal to compromise in matters of Christian Socialist principle to tramp the byways of Yorkshire and to turn his hand to any small bit of mending or making good to earn a living. There was a black mark of radicalism against his name and that meant he was always fired from a job as soon as his reputation caught up with him. He would leave Scarborough before dawn every Monday morning and tramp from parish to parish with a blanket and a sack of tools on his back, looking for work, and his family would see him again when he returned with a few shillings in his pocket the following Saturday night – always to a musical evening, for everyone in the family played an instrument.

However, in Auckland things changed. Among the jobs that used his talents as an artist and craftsman was a two-year stint making the joinery for, and handcarving the interior of, the beautiful little Catholic church on the road running up to Parnell. But he was far more than just a wonder-worker with his hands. Inside him was something of a frustrated poet. And he was a first-class fantasist, with a secret taste in dreadful junk.

It was one of the great thrills of my childhood to be a witness to my father's raids on his father's stores of treasure. He would unscrew the door or prise open a window of the double-locked little bach – or sleep-out, as it would now be called – at the back of our house, where the old man lived alone. Then he'd break open the padlocked lids of the boxes and, to furious cries of 'Look at this, will you! What would the old bastard want with twenty-six pairs of spectacles he can't even see through?' or 'What the hell is he doing with seven assorted artificial limbs?', my father would fling armfuls of junk around the room, to be swept up later and burnt on a garden fire or taken away to the dump.

The range of Henry Marflitt's interests was extraordinary. There would be tracts on converting heathen savages to exotic Christian sects, teapot lids minus their teapots, alarming books of advice on intimate medical problems (with diagrams), stereoscopic seaside postcards complete with hand-held viewers, pamphlets with illustrations explaining the curious mechanics and processes of electric or galvanic therapy, ancient dolls, peculiar devices used for colonic irrigation, opera glasses, human hair, pocket knives, press cuttings, coloured pens and pencils, mind-boggling items of intimate clothing, job lots of ill-fitting and unsaleable shoes, sets of false teeth with gums the colour of congealed blood, starched collars, costume jewellery, watches that wouldn't work, patent remedies, ostrich feathers, and tools, tools, tools – some of them of perfect utilitarian beauty, but many in their original oilpaper wrappers, never used. In one large box we uncovered a full brand-new Stanley combination plane, with all its huge array of amazing blades and moulding devices. It was worth a fortune, in his terms – so how had the old boy come by it?

I remember once seeing Henry Marflitt return home to discover that his treasure hoard had yet again been looted and destroyed by his youngest son, and watching him burst into silent uncontrollable tears while my father lectured him about how as a child the family had been forced to eat bread and dripping, and had always lived in rented shacks in Freeman's Bay, while the boxes under the house kept filling with useless junk.

Undoubtedly my father had a point, but I remember those tears with horror. I had never before witnessed an adult in the grip of true grief. And I had not been aware till that moment that anyone could cry without making the slightest sound.

The day's glorious raid instantly lost its magic. I thought my father cruel. It was one of those small but shattering revelations about the grown-up world that you never quite recover from.

For a junk collector, Henry Marflitt was unusually orderly. Most leave their odds and ends strewn and tumbling all over the place, but his gleanings were always wrapped and boxed up neatly, as if to have them available for immediate negotiation in the trash trade.

He also had three other interesting quirks that I remember clearly. The first was that he never drank tea out of a cup. He would always pour the fluid into his saucer and slurp it up through his moustache. No amount of pleading would induce him to change the habit of a lifetime. He simply preferred tea that way. 'Aerated,' he called it.

The second was that his bach always smelled of overripe bananas. He would store them in a cupboard until their skins turned black and their substance became runny before devouring them.

And the third was that he took his politics super-seriously. He used to compose long letters to cabinet ministers in the first Labour government, supplying them with free advice on how to run their departments and the country in general.

Henry Marflitt was extremely proud of the formal printed notices he received from the ministers' secretaries in return, thanking him for writing. To him it was confirmation that our politicians could never have managed without him.

My paternal grandfather died by double misadventure. Even on the pension he used to take a packed lunch to town, as though he were still heading off to work. Mostly, however, he spent his time reading, or writing his letters to politicians, in public libraries, though if it was a sunny day he would sometimes be spotted by embarrassed family members sitting down by the wharves, chatting, reading newspapers or just eating his lunch and throwing the crusts to the seagulls. But every so often he'd pick up odd jobs around town, mainly for old ladies, in whom he had an irremediable interest and for whom he worked for very little or, often enough, nothing.

One of the crazier of these women egged him on, when he was seventy-eight, to cut back her enormous front hedge. It was work for a very fit young man, but the woman insisted that Henry Marflitt have a go at it just to please and impress her – which he was only too eager to do. So she also provided him with a rotten ladder, just to help make the job exciting and dangerous.

Of course, the ladder collapsed and Henry Marflitt ended up in Auckland hospital with a broken thigh bone. He was a wiry old sod and made a good recovery, and as soon as he got out of bed he resumed his trips to town with the workers. But coming home one evening he made the fatal mistake of trying to dash across the road in front of the

UNDER THE BRIDGE & OVER THE MOON

bus. A car collected him, breaking his thigh bone again, and this time he died in hospital.

The poor woman who ran him down suffered terribly over an accident that was no fault of hers. She gave up driving, had nightmares and went into an incurable nervous decline.

And as if that wasn't bad enough, his death was also given lasting disfigurement by some neighbours called Scott. They were the only household nearby with a telephone, so my father gave their number to the hospital for use in an emergency.

Mr Scott, who was a prize fart of the first order of gentility, knocked one evening on our front door to ask my father, whose name he pretended suddenly not to know, if he happened to be the person who had given his private number to the Auckland hospital.

'Yes,' my father said, and explained the circumstances.

'Well then,' Mr Scott announced, 'your father is dead, and in future would you please not feel free to use my phone in this way.'

4: THE COLONEL AND HIS LADY

When I was nineteen I decided to write down the brilliant tales of the strange background and bizarre adventures of my maternal grandfather, Joseph McKenney. It was going to be my first book, and there would be nothing to it. All I had to do was sit beside him and copy out the stories as they poured out of him. Or so I thought.

It took me years to learn that writing seldom comes that easily. But in any case my decision was both too soon and too late, for he died that same year and the record remains only in my memory, and in a larger remembrance of life and family that I luckily got my mother to commit to paper about twenty-five years later.

Where my mother and I diverge occasionally in the minor detail of the record, I have favoured my own version of what happened, for I don't feel an obligation to defer to her subtle narrative colourings and flagrant self-justifications – though I think I can now understand them.

So far as I am concerned, the deciding factor is that at times I feel closer to the truth because these deeply personal stories were the only ones that my grandfather would relate without alteration, whereas he embroidered all his other tales, not just because it would have bored him to tell exactly the same story twice, but because he was a genius of the spoken word and couldn't help elaborating and adding to and decorating as his inspiration or the mood of the moment took him.

The record, whichever way you look at it, shows that my mother's family, the McKenneys, were quite as mad as the Jowseys, though in utterly different ways. My mother's McKinney grandparents (for the name was spelt that way until her father, who was born and died a McKinney, followed local pronunciation and replaced the i with an e on his marriage certificate and daughters' birth certificates) had arrived from Ireland in the early 1860s, and rather fancied themselves in the same presumptuous manner that all royals, nobles, tribal chiefs, dignitaries and even some amateur genealogists adopt: they proceeded from the absurd notion that they possessed a 'history' as a family and, therefore, were better born than others.

In fact, though my mother's McKinney grandmother came from a family that for some generations had been able to afford a Catholic French education – which stopped just short of herself and her nearest sister, for the terrible famine of 1846 intervened – and though she exalted in a lineage that she could recite backwards for more than a thousand years, to rival any kuia, and though she called herself a McCarthy of Desmond, and a Fitzgerald, and the family boasted a very pretty-looking little castle which inside was as dank and unhealthy as any other, she became, some time after her husband's death, no more, if no less, than the proprietor of a wooden hostelry in Frasertown at the back of Poverty Bay – though she would have it known that it was a large and prosperous one.

The accommodation and liquor trade must have suited her well, despite her claim to breeding and the impediment of a brood of seven children, for after the death of her first husband – my great-grandfather, Mathew McKinney – she eventually remarried, to a man called Darvill, and shifted to Sydney where, I believe, she was soon set up again with some kind of guest house or hotel.

Mathew McKinney was the colonel of an Irish regiment stationed in India. The money for his commission and, before that, for a university education for himself and his brother (who became what my grandfather gloried in referring to as 'the world champion at the single sculls'), came from a Belfast family business specialising in agricultural machinery. The Belfast McKinneys, by the way, maintained a close connection with their American cousins, who were successful brewers – a relationship with the bottle that has seldom proved profitable to the family, for it has managed to afflict, and often curse and destroy, at least one victim in every generation.

Mathew was a terrible self-destructive drunk, yet his love for the bottle was actually to save the lives of his family in the strangest possible circumstances. Setting out for New Zealand, via Australia, he went on a final pub crawl, missed the boat and had to catch another. When he eventually got to the newly founded Napier, he discovered that the first ship had sunk with no survivors.

The colonel moved inland to the armed constabulary post at Frasertown, but did no more than play a peculiarly colourful and non-active part in the wars at the time, when he found himself temporarily, though memorably, in charge. His garrison was paid a surprise visit by some army panjandrum, and my great-grandfather and his major were discovered to be entirely obliterated by liquor, and most of their troops in no better condition. Family legend has it that he was fond of the army life because it provided almost endless opportunity for getting drunk.

Following that fiasco, and in a half-hearted search for other occupations suitable to his station in life, Mathew managed to get himself appointed local sheriff – for a whole day. However, he resigned immediately he was told that one of his duties was to supervise hangings. Shooting the enemy was one thing, but stringing up a man in cold blood was no line of business for an officer and Irish gentleman of good breeding and classical education.

During his short life in Hawke's Bay and Poverty Bay Mathew McKinney devoted most of his energies to an extraordinary thirst, and whatever time was left over was lavished on fast and high-spirited horses, which were roughly equivalent in their attraction to the sports cars which were eventually to replace them, and which have proved no less lethal.

Drunk and devil-may-care, he boasted one day that he could swim a horse across the Wairoa River in spate, and accepted a five-pound bet to prove the fact. As it happened, however, his opinion of his abilities could not have been more wrong. He was swept away and his body was recovered several miles down-river.

I was much intrigued, as a small boy, as to whether or not the lost wager was ever paid, but my grandfather was no real help in solving the problem. Sometimes he would answer that of course the debt would have been squared up, as a matter of honour. Yet as often as not, he would say his father had paid with his life and no gambling man would ever have dared stand before the widow and demand the price of the wager as well.

The colonel's name does not appear on the list of drownings – the 'New Zealand death' as it was called – that was kept pretty meticulously at the time, but the story was well attested by all sides of the family, which makes me think that Church influence may have been brought to bear to conceal the scandalous and almost suicidal aspect of the escapade, and to put his demise down to some other misadventure.

Although a cousin of mine spent a great deal of time and trouble trying to locate our great-grandfather's death certificate, he was unable ever to come up with one. It seems to have been mislaid, lost or destroyed. So I am inclined to set some store by my maternal grandfather's account of being taken as a boy of five to witness the macabre disinterment of the colonel's carefully buried corpse from unconsecrated ground and his re-interment in the local churchyard. The implications of this incident support a theory that the family strove strenuously to have the truth suppressed and that it managed, after a safe and decent time had elapsed, to have its efforts ceremonially endorsed by the Church.

Incidentally, since my maternal grandfather was born posthumously, the only time that he was ever to gaze upon his father's face was on that day of horror, when the coffin lid was lifted and the seals of the inner casket were broken, and he was compelled to inspect the colonel's remains after they had lain five years in the ground.

He described the scene to me once only, and refused to discuss it ever again. The first thought that struck him, he told me, was how his father looked like a picture he had seen of a monkey. The whole face seemed covered in hair, and it was only explained to the boy later that this was because the skin had shrunk so that the hair follicles had been forced out. Then, he said, as he was watching in fear and fascination, there was a terrible moment when the face suddenly began to shiver then seemed to turn to jelly – an illusion brought about by a general disintegration as the outside air hit the body. The sight of his dead father haunted him for the rest of his life.

Until she was able to set up business renting rooms and selling beer in her Frasertown hostelry, Mathew's widow had a tough time of it. At first there was hope of the McKinney children inheriting the immense fortune, estimated at one hundred thousand pounds, of Mathew's relative 'Aunt' Berry, a childless Hawke's Bay Catholic lady. However, as she lay dying, the Church arrived in force, there was no getting near the place for priests, nuns and even the bishop, and the will was changed in its favour – an eventuality that is said to have brought on a furious outbreak of atheism among the older children.

But, more sinisterly, there was whisper of my great-grandmother's rape by some Maoris, possibly Ngati Porou, possibly Te Kooti's men, and an innuendo that persisted throughout his eighty-plus years that my maternal grandfather was issue of that act. However, since the suggestion is not provable and since his birth certificate attests that his name was Joseph McKinney, it is prudent to follow the advice of the very sensible old saying and agree that he was, after all, no better and no worse than the son of his father – even if the story does highlight one of the genuine perils, as well as one of the not unusual rogue rumours, of the period.

At any rate, and for whatever now-unfathomable reason, my great-grandmother showed nothing but psychotic loathing for her youngest child, and Joseph was given into the supervision of an older brother, who neglected his duties so badly that the small child was more often taken in and cared for by local Ngati Porou, though every now and again his mother would fly into an insane rage at the thought of him, and his brothers and sisters would be sent out to round him up and bring him 'home' so that he could receive a corrective flogging. One hopes these did her the world of good before the boy crawled back to the Ngati Porou.

Her most impressive act of torture was to have my grandfather, at the age of eight, tied to her favourite whipping-post, an iron bedstead, so that she could attempt to flay him alive – this time with a length of wire. When he told me of this ordeal, my grandfather explained that I was not to believe that his mother was so unnatural that she had flogged him with a wire whip *intentionally*, because it had always been her habit to thrash him with whatever piece of timber or hardware was closest to hand, and it was probably just his bad luck that the wire had been lying by the bed.

He always described his mother to me as 'a mad and vicious bitch out of hell' and he hated her as much as she abominated him, though once, through curiosity and perhaps some vain and lingering hope for affection, he went looking for her, nearly twenty years after that final merciless and deranged thrashing, in Sydney – only to discover that there were now two Darvill children, both loved as tenderly as he had never been, to add to the seven McKinneys she had left behind in New Zealand.

The outcome of his ordeal by wire whip was that my grandfather at last understood that his life was in danger and he used his wits to keep entirely out of his mother's orbit until she eventually left for Australia when he was ten. During this time he worked for his tucker on a bullock team, as a goad-boy, and became a swearing boozing urchin of the roads around Poverty Bay. Like his father before him, he also developed a passion for fast horses and became an amateur jockey at country race meetings – until he grew too big and heavy, and had to turn his hand to mustering on sheep stations, working teams of horses, and horse-breaking and training. Also, like many fit young men at the time, he was able to fill in with an axe and saw, for there were usually plenty of jobs to be found in the bush.

In his mid twenties he went to Australia, where he spent some years 'humping his bluey' – on the swag – searching for work from station to station, then prospecting for gold, mainly around Coolgardie and Kalgoorlie. But he also spent time in New South Wales, where he hung about with Henry Lawson and his coterie, and where he met Harry Holland, the future head of the New Zealand Labour Party, in prison.

Eventually, in Queensland, he contracted malaria, followed by a near-fatal bout of trichinosis, and he returned to New Zealand where, through his own efforts at self-education and self-improvement, he was accepted as an insurance salesman on the West Coast, working for the AMP, with a doctor called Charlie Morcain in tow, before moving on to richer pastures in the insurance business in Feilding, then in Hawera, indulging a taste for swank suits and fine creamy ponies, before concluding his life's enterprises as a failed farmer at Whangamomona.

Till his dying day my grandfather would advance the Collected Pronouncements of Dr Charlie Morcain as the last word on every aspect of medicine. God knows where such a paragon acquired his knowledge, but I can attest that no particularity of scientific wisdom or intimate advice was beyond the good doctor's judgement, though it was often argued angrily by my mother and her sisters that the man was a hundred years out of date, that his opinions were a public danger and that he

UNDER THE BRIDGE & OVER THE MOON

was owed a very qualified homage only for being the agent of fate that brought their parents together.

It was Dr Morcain who introduced the couple who were to become my maternal grandfather and grandmother, at a social gathering in Kumara, on the West Coast. He was thus responsible, in a metaphoric sense, for delivering a long line of descendants, including myself, into the world.

5: MAC

Joseph McKenney may indeed have grown up to be a thoroughly ballsed-up muddle of a man, but he was also the undisputed hero and champion of my childhood, the greatest bullshitting storyteller, balladmonger and baritone show-off I've ever met or heard of. I loved him more than I ever loved my parents. I was spellbound by him; I absolutely adored him.

He never allowed anyone to call him by his proper name or by an honorific. He stamped on all mention of Joe, Dad or Granddad. To his wife, daughters, grandchildren and everyone else he met, he was just plain Mac.

The man was bald, walnut brown and six foot tall, built athletically, like a wedge, from his broad muscular shoulders and barrel chest to slim hips and extraordinarily fine-boned size-six feet – of which he was excessively proud, for he truly believed that only 'natural' aristocrats were born with mudhooks of such high-arched, small-sized distinction. Although an early photograph shows him as having the fairly cleancut features of a man about town, the older he grew the rounder and darker his face became.

Because of his strange upbringing, Mac spoke Maori equally as well as English, and for some years of his childhood, when he was cared for largely by the Frasertown iwi, his first language was Maori. Several times, in the middle of Auckland, I saw him approached in the street and addressed directly by Maori who were convinced that he belonged to one of the tribes.

I suppose Mac's rig-out, as well as his natural deep tan, also had a lot to do with it. He would never venture out on the street, even to go to the corner for a newspaper or a threepenny cigar, without wearing a bowler hat, chewing on a pipe, often unlit, and wielding a walking stick. He didn't mind appearing in public in a buttoned-up pink woollen singlet instead of a shirt, but without a bowler, pipe and stick – never on your life. For him, it would have been like walking down the street naked.

My favourite story of his Maoriness is my mother's account of travelling with her father on the Main Trunk railway. An elderly and distinguished-looking Maori man, accompanied by a young Maori woman, boarded the train and sat in the seat facing them at the end of the carriage.

Because the two men were accompanied by attractive young women of different races, there was a slight embarrassment between them and their conversation began in a desultory way, without the usual preliminary exchange of courtesies about where they hailed from. As the train headed south, however, their conversation, which was entirely in Maori, grew more animated. But it was only when it came time for the Maori gentleman to leave the train that he asked my grandfather the delayed but important question of which tribe he belonged to.

'Ngati Porou,' was my grandfather's proud prompt reply.

My mother knew the language imperfectly, but well enough to understand what her father had just said and to recognise that he had told what seemed to her to be a lie.

'Goodness!' she objected, when they were alone. 'Should you have claimed to be Ngati Porou like that?'

Mac replied: 'Well, what the hell else could I do? I couldn't humiliate a decent chap like that by letting on I was no Maori, when he hadn't picked it for himself. Anyway, and another thing, a goddamned hard time I'd have had when I was young if it hadn't been for the Ngati Porou. They fed and looked after me like one of themselves in times when my own people couldn't have cared a bugger or less if I had perished or gone to hell. I *feel* Ngati Porou.'

Besides the two sons who died in infancy, one after a few days and the other after some months, my maternal grandparents had four daughters, none of whom was much use around the rugged hills at the back of the farm. Like the quintessentially English names of my father's siblings, Mac's daughters bore names that reflected the Irishness of both parents: Doreen (which was my mother's first name, though she was always known as Clare), Moya, Kathleen (who was always known as Biddy) and Sheila.

My mother, vengefully – and against all the physical and biographical evidence – always referred to her father as puny (though not in her written account of the family history), for throughout her life she conducted a private war with him (though not strictly *against* him), I suspect largely on the grounds that she wanted not so much to defeat him as to cut him down to size. She deeply resented the way I hero-worshipped him – a thing she had not been able to do as a child, for she was never able to absolve him for his wickedness in taking her away from a good and prosperous life in Feilding, where she had been born, and for casting her adored high-spirited mother in a grinding backblocks role as a farmer's wife, once he had successfully courted and captivated her with an appearance of wealth and sober style – which was as valid a criticism of him, I suppose, as the first grudge against my love for him was unreasonable.

Mac could put on the greatest one-man show I've ever seen, without needing a single foil or prop. His private performances ranged from low comedy to high tragedy, for he recognised intuitively what so few actors ever get into their skulls – that there's a very small gap between the two: perhaps no more than a look, a short pause, a fleeting gesture or a fall in the voice. He had a wonderful brain and a phenomenal memory – probably because it hadn't been buggered about with by the wrong sort of schooling. As a child, he had never spent a day in a classroom, and he had had to teach himself to read and write. Consequently, his mind was brimming with all sorts of unusual gleanings and odd juxtapositions that had never been 'educated' out of him.

My grandfather's boast was that he could recite poetry non-stop every evening for a week without repeating himself, and if you included his huge repertoire of songs, he would not have been far short of the mark. He only had to hear a song once to catch the words and tune forever, and he committed to memory all the long poems of Burns and a lot of the shorter ones, a canto of *Don Juan*, among a huge store of Byron's other poems, the whole of *The Rime of the Ancient Mariner*, the complete Fitzgerald version of *The Rubáiyát of Omar Khayyám*, screeds and screeds of Henry Lawson and a fair amount of Banjo Paterson, plus an assortment of other verses comical and heroical. The performances were stunning: songs, poems and stories, one leading to another as the mood took him and as he assessed the reaction of his audiences.

When (as I shall soon relate) I went to live with him for almost two years as a child, I can remember night after night, when we had eaten dinner, climbing his chair in front of the kitchen range and curling up like a cat on his lap. I would rest my head on his chest and feel the rich and sonorous vibrations of his words rumble through me as he launched into song and recitation, and I would lie there in perfect rapture, inhabiting the articulation of his words, until I would feel my whole being dissolve into the living power of his imagination.

However, it was an experience that stopped just short of the authentically mystical, for now that I think about it, part of the explanation for the state of ecstasy into which his recitations transported me may also have had something to do with the probability that I was half-giddy from breathing the heady aromatic fragrance of his cigars and the dark Tasman plug he used to carve off a block of tobacco with a sharp pocket knife, rub in the cupped palms of his hands, stuff into his pipe and burn in great gusts of smoke that glowed grey-blue, like luminous clouds of night, below the flitting yellow moon of the electric light bulb.

But Mac's greatest shows were the impromptu performances that he would give, years later, when he would suddenly turn up at home for lunch at the weekend – for those were the days, before the telephone, when relatives and friends would just 'arrive' on the doorstep and expect to be fed.

He would wait till the meal was about three quarters over before dropping what would sound like some casual remark about, say, a man he'd spotted that very same day, sitting in the back seat of a Dominion Road tram, who had one ear, one arm and one leg only, and all on his right side – in fact, he would declare, here was a specimen of man you could fairly describe as having no proper left side to his body.

As children, we were absolute suckers for these brilliant attention-grabbers. We would instantly start arguing the correctness or wrongness of leftness and rightness, or whatever absurdity Mac had planted in our brains, and we'd soon talk ourselves into a total whirl, where we'd be in a perfect state for his next move, which would be to introduce some extraordinary character or incident from the past that would only add to our confusion. This, in turn, would lead to further elaborations and embellishments, and eventually to vast bizarre arabesques of storytelling that would sweep us all away with their faultless magic.

Sometimes the tales were tragic and gruesome; often they were heart-stopping with perils; but mostly they would start off with some small sly

UNDER THE BRIDGE & OVER THE MOON

piece of nonsense and build up into wild and outrageous lunacies that would have us screaming with laughter. Many's the time Mac had us actually weeping and rolling about the floor, terrified that we'd be sick or choke to death in spasms of comic hysteria.

And it wasn't just the children. As I write these words I can still see my father, with tears of laughter rolling down his cheeks, beating his fists on the table and yelling, 'Stop. Stop. Stop. I'm going to bloody die.'

Mac was a poet himself, though I've never been able to work out why no one could ever get him to recite his own verses – just some of the wonderfully inventive lines he would make up to replace the banal ditties that accompanied the popular tunes of the day. But I do know that he constructed wooden hoardings on his properties at Whanga-momona, on which he daubed his poems in big bold letters.

It has always struck me as one of the most interesting clues to the inner workings of this complex marvel of a man that he should paint his poems as though they were to be understood as being part of the landscape; that he should do so for an audience largely of cattle and sheep; and that by using wooden boards instead of paper as his writing medium he should attempt to remove poetry's single technical advantage over all the other arts – its portability.

If only I could convince the art world that Colin McCahon, as a young artist searching for a breakthrough, drove through Whanga-momona one day in the 1930s and saw those huge hoardings with words painted all over them and thought to himself, 'Now, there's a bright idea just waiting for someone to come along and pick it up . . .'

6: GOING WEST

Mac's wife, Margaret – my maternal grandmother – was born on the West Coast. Her father's name was Michael Rouse. The surname is associated with the West of England and is found commonly enough in Devon and Cornwall, though in an Irish context it indicates, I am told, that some forgotten ancestor may have embarked at some time for the southern parts of Ireland, possibly even with Carew's

Elizabethan adventurers and land speculators, which is the polite term for a gang of royal bandits. The Irish can gaze at you knowingly and read a whole history of likely associations into the surname that you may have thought had no more relevance than a tag tied to a suitcase.

Margaret's mother was a Davern, which is of passing curiosity for those interested in remote New Zealand literary relationships, as it appears in several other forms, including Davin. Indeed, it amused Dan Davin, when I used to call on him in Oxford in the 1970s, to speculate on the possibility of some distant crossing of genes, though the story of the Daverns and the Rouses is both far stranger and far easier to attest than a long shot of that kind.

Michael Rouse is said to have arrived in the South Island of New Zealand in the 1850s and to have worked his way from Dunedin across Otago to the West Coast, following the gold trail, although it has seemed to me more probable that it was merely his destiny to be afflicted with that compass in the heart which had steered so many generations of Rouses in westerly directions.

A brother, similarly guided towards points westward, became a professor of Latin at an American university, though it was not his academic prowess that secured him lasting fame among his relatives, but the manner of his death, which was nothing short of sensational. The Latinist died from ptomaine poisoning contracted by consuming a tin of badly blown salmon. His end was still being cited, to his great-grand-nieces and nephews, including myself, nearly a century later. The ghastly clinical details were a terrible warning to us concerning the perils of eating tinned food, and the stuff was seldom allowed to be brought into the house.

The New Zealand Rouse made a substantial living out of one of the essential items of equipment that made the goldrushes possible in the hard South Island climate and terrain – boots. During the West Coast gold rush Michael's best handmade boots cost the enormous sum of five pounds a pair, but he believed proudly that there were none better in the land, and a constant queue of customers supported the view.

He was a man much concerned with pride in other directions too. He never sent more than one bill to a genuine Coaster for his products, on the grounds that if they couldn't afford them they were welcome to them and if they were too dishonest to pay the same sentiment applied as well.

There is a family legend, often repeated, that Michael acquired some sort of official status in the running of Hokitika and handled matters so

UNDER THE BRIDGE & OVER THE MOON

well that he was asked to apply for the position of Town Clerk in Christchurch. The story sounds to me as though it is more likely to have been true of Michael's second son, Rob, who was actually roped into Council responsibility in Kumara when the family moved there. However all that may be, the joke of the legend is that this splendid opportunity for family advancement was spurned disdainfully on the grounds that the West Coast had vast reserves of as yet undiscovered gold, and therefore a far more brilliant future than Canterbury – one of the many errors of judgement that still run in the blood and consistently afflict the Rouse descendants.

Little has been remembered of Michael's wife Bridget – for she was not of the bloodline that was to descend through my mother's mother, a circumstance that I shall soon clarify – except that she earned a reputation for endurance by bearing a dozen babies, most of whom died in infancy. Only four of her children survived.

My mother described Michael, her grandfather, as impetuous and strong-minded, which seems to me a bit on the mild side for a man who, despite his status as a citizen of substance, got himself arrested for demonstrating over the hanging of the Manchester Martyrs, and earned notoriety by marching into the local Catholic school, seizing the cane from a schoolteacher and flogging him in front of his class for his desperate moral depravity in whacking Michael's son Tom, then aged twelve, for not informing on a fellow pupil – this to an Irishman, for whom the wickedness of informing was often declared to be the sin against the Holy Spirit that would land you in hell for all eternity and could never be forgiven.

Deluded by notions of uncompromising scorn, Irish resentment, self-righteousness and lunatic grandeur, living in a wild setting, far from the tormented homeland he had left as part of the diaspora that followed the Great Famine, and now having set himself up as a businessman of civic repute among a drifting population of gold-mad dreamers, my irascible great-grandfather Michael found himself at the age of forty-five with money in the bank, but in a condition of gloomy loneliness, suddenly made worse by his enforced separation from the company of women by the death of his wife.

The puritan poverty of spirit that distinguishes Irish Catholicism from its more humane Mediterranean counterpart added to the misery – so who would not believe that here was a soul fettered by a set of values and social circumstances ripe for anarchic overthrow?

Anarchy duly arrived in the form of his seventeen-year-old relative Bridget Davern, who had arrived in the colony in 1875 from Ballylanders in County Limerick, four years prior to the death of her namesake, Bridget Rouse.

And since this was a very Irish development, a brief digression into the background is required to understand the characters involved and the circumstances that oppressed them. Young Bridget Davern had emigrated from Ireland with her elder sister Margaret, one of several relatives for whom Michael Rouse had stumped up the fare to enable them to escape poverty in Ireland – as was the expected duty of all those who had got out and made good.

Centuries earlier, the interloping Rouses had married into the Daverns, whose ancestors had lived in the West of Ireland, in Clare, Limerick and Tipperary in particular, as far back as memory would allow, which was all the way to the deepest recesses of recorded time. At first the Daverns proved a useful connection, for Ballylanders, where they owned valuable property, is near the head of what is called the Golden Vale, one of the lushest belts of emerald land in the whole of Ireland. But now the Rouses were in a position to return all favours, for the times were desperate. That this area had become a corner of the wasteland of the Great Famine, or that it could be part of a general scene of rural poverty, seems almost impossible to believe when you look at it today, but this is what happened, and it still provides the substance of old and complex Irish grievances.

When my mother, in her retirement, visited the County Limerick birthplace of her grandmother, Bridget Davern, a whole hundred years after Bridget's departure for New Zealand by sailing ship at the age of fourteen or fifteen, the story of all that had occurred to that young woman on the far West Coast of New Zealand so long ago was known and still being talked about in detail on the other side of the world. It was as though everything had taken place just outside the environs of the town itself – and hardly more than yesterday.

My mother described her arrival back among the Daverns as being treated like a member of the family who'd been off, say, on a trip to visit friends in Cork, or perhaps a long weekend's shopping expedition to Dublin. Hers was a perfectly normal and everyday 'homecoming' for them. Time didn't come into it, and no one expressed surprise or made a particular fuss. My mother was simply restored to the circle of her relatives, which included the very real presence of those buried in the graveyard.

It was the reverse of the Rip Van Winkle story, for it was as though the clocks had stood still in the town and my mother had wandered in out of another age.

Faced with that same prospect a few years later, I got my wife to stop the car and photograph me at the signpost just outside the town of Ballylanders, to prove I'd been there. Then we drove in one side and slowly out the other with our windows wound up.

I wanted to get a good glimpse at what was now a pleasant and prosperous-looking place, not a bit like the image handed down by my great-grandparents. I had no desire to get out and meet my distant relatives as my mother had done, for all the time I had the feeling that, if awakened, the long memories of the Irish might reach out and drag me down into some terrible pit of ancient trespass and commotion.

7: 'NOW, GODS, STAND UP FOR BASTARDS!'

The death of Michael's wife in 1879 meant a woman was badly needed in the Rouse household, for although the two surviving boys were seventeen and twenty-two respectively, and were therefore as good as grown up, the two daughters were not old enough to look after themselves. Ellen, the younger, was only six.

Seventeen-year-old Bridget Davern was summoned from Nelson to take charge. The arrangement whereby some female relative, old or young, was obliged to fill the gap left by the death of a wife and mother was a common enough one in Irish families at the time, for it was the most practical (and the cheapest) way of coping with the enormous and fairly primitive daily labours of cooking, washing, cleaning, organising and caring. What was possibly less conventional was that Bridget's duties soon also involved becoming the bed-companion to her 'fatherly' forty-five-year-old blood relative.

The arrangement was explained to me once by my mother as being based on free choice. It was said that the pair loved each other without coercion and in full understanding of what they were doing – and there is no reason why this should not have been so, and indeed, since there are no facts to contradict the statement, none should doubt it.

But their general situation should also be taken into account, not through prurience, but for its own historical interest. Michael and Bridget could never marry. It is thought that they were uncle and niece, though they may have been first cousins, but whatever their exact relationship, it is enough to say that it was so close that it was within the church's 'forbidden degrees of kindred'. Michael was a prominent citizen of middle age, whereas Bridget's social standing was confined to the shadow cast by her 'protector'; and she was still a minor. In fact, the only area – except the bedroom – in which they were not to consider themselves fettered by circumstance was their faith. They were both devout Catholics.

However, that was not the end of the problems they faced as a very unlikely couple. Matters were made infinitely worse by booze. From the onset of his wife's last illness, Michael Rouse had begun to drink like a draught horse. His thriving boot business went to hell, the money disappeared with it, and when he died at the age of fifty-two, he was as good as bankrupt.

In eight years Michael had been completely cleaned out – and this was the man who had been able to settle a cool five hundred quid in cash on Bridget's elder sister Margaret, to help her have a fit of failed memory when writing back home and never to mention the scandalous matter of what he and Bridget were up to in bed.

It was more money wasted – for, as I have explained, word got back to Ireland all right – but at least Margaret and her husband knew what to do with a sum of that magnitude. They put it straight into a pub on a Central Otago crossroads, where they had the good fortune to benefit from one of the false gold rushes that sprang from hope and rumour, and they soon made enough to be able to purchase one of the South Island's biggest high-country sheep stations.

Two years before he died, Michael Rouse became father to a daughter he and Bridget named Margaret, after her aunt. She is my 'Rouse' grandmother.

Soon after Michael's death the two Rouse sons moved the family from Hokitika to Kumara, where they revived the footwear business, and where Bridget established a dominant position as matriarch; but neither man ever married.

In his middle age, for reasons unknown, the elder son, Tom, just packed up one day, went on his travels around the country and simply melted away into a Maori community somewhere in the North Island. Because this move was a matter of free will, it seemed to cause neither consternation nor even surprise, but what really did provoke a tremendous scandal back in Kumara was a subsequent report that Tom Rouse, a West Coast Catholic gentleman, had been seen in the north gobbling raw huhu grubs.

As my mother commented later, 'A Rouse might slight the moral code and the world must swallow it,' but the world did not have to accept that 'a Rouse literally swallowed grubs'. Family pride – quite literally – feasts wonderfully off such refinements and distinctions.

The second son, Rob, who was reputed to be the second white child born on the West Coast and was altogether a genial good man, devoted his life to the welfare of his dependants: his two young sisters, his 'aunt' Bridget (who was the same age as himself) and his baby half-sister Margaret – plus, in some way or other, it seemed, just about everyone else in town.

In the strange puritan Irish fashion of the day, his life's duties were respectability, strict self-denial and absolute responsibility – and these were only to be expected of him. In the circumstances, celibacy was to be Rob's fate; there was no question of his taking a wife.

The elder Rouse daughter died at sixteen and unfortunately the younger, Ellen, was as ugly and miserable as her dead sister had been radiantly beautiful. She was a poor creature, who bent her whole existence to becoming the town shrew of Kumara. Of Michael's five surviving children, the four born in wedlock failed to have issue. The only fertile line was the bastard one.

8: A VOLUPTUOUS CUNNING

Frank Sargeson once showed me, in a book he was reading, a photograph of an elderly, dumpy and decidedly unattractive Frieda Weekley, who as a stifled yet radiant and still youngish woman had abandoned her husband and three children to run off with D. H.

Lawrence. Frank's comment was, 'Makes you wonder what all the fuss was about, doesn't it?'

Well, yes, of course I had to agree, though I managed to make some comment about how the same sort of wisdom was sooner or later going to make all of us look as though we'd fallen out of our prams and flat on our dials when we were young.

But it's the same unfair way that I now view the only photograph that my mother has given me of Bridget Davern, in her mid to late forties, standing beside her twenty-something-year-old daughter Margaret Rouse. You have to shut out the image of the older woman and study the face of the daughter to get any sort of clue as to how Michael Rouse could have been so crazed with desire that he would flout the expectations of his children, the proprieties of his bourgeois neighbours, Victorian convention and the strict codes of the Church itself. Bridget dominates her share of the frame, hideously majestic in her widow's weeds, as though she is in training to go fifteen rounds with the Devil himself – and only a fool would bet even money on his chances against her.

She is formidable in every sense of the word. She and Michael tried only to avoid causing a scandal back in Ireland, but so far as the Coast was concerned, there were to be no concessions. They made no attempt to conceal their sleeping arrangements, and no neighbour or priest ever challenged them on the subject. And when Bridget died she was buried in honour beside Michael and his wife, after one of the grandest funerals Hokitika had ever seen. I ended a poem I wrote her some years ago, and which I called without a trace of irony 'A Founder of the Nation', in these words:

And, though

the Irish are a remembering tribe and skilled
at casting the first stone, who will now recollect
of that vast metropolis of gold-mad ghosts

the moonlight seduction of a teenage,
immigrant girl by a guardian old enough
to be her father? She was right,

there had been too much running away,
she had come far enough and now she would challenge
the times: See me as I judge. The portrait

> that remains testifies to trials and strengths.
> It takes nerve deriving from her own to detect
> in her glance the shadow of a voluptuous cunning.

I still hold with that last line. And if I were now able to answer Frank Sargeson's question now, I think I'd put it that way and no other. Frieda Weekley, Bridget Davern, my own mother, and all the other thousands of women who kick over the traces every year are doomed, with average good health, to grow old, and the young may certainly wonder at what anyone once saw in them. But that's the job of the imagination. In the shadows of the wrinkles there is almost always the ghost suggestion of the voluptuous cunning that drove them to tear up the whole book of rules and challenge the times.

I don't believe there's anything necessarily admirable in their behaviour. In fact, the results can sometimes seem merely callous, self-infatuated and indifferent to the lives of others, and perhaps even despicable or harmful. But I do believe that, when circumstances provide a trigger, there's an assertive force that will not be denied in the most repressed or even the mildest of people. It is as creative and potentially full of poems as it is destructive and eager to tear its victims limb from limb – and it bides its time in all of us.

Which is, I have to confess, a circuitous way of getting around to the subject of my mother, a woman whose life has been as absurd, wilful, productive, dramatic, heartless, self-indulgent and thoroughly inexcusable as any I know.

My first clear memory of her can be pinpointed precisely to the eighteenth of February 1936, the day before my brother Anthony is to be born in a small Royal Oak maternity hospital.

I am two years and six months old, and my father and I are standing there, beside my mother's bed, and I am struck by the great mountain of her belly rising under a white counterpane.

I can't remember having noticed her pregnancy before, but what must have seemed a quite unremarkable and gradual increase in girth in our home is somehow made to seem extraordinary in this strange place and beneath such unusual bedclothes. More than sixty years later I can still recall asking her in the maternity hospital how she came to be so fat and her telling me the sensational news that she was about to have a baby.

My next memory is in full colour and I can still follow it like a movie, from scene to scene, as it unfolds. The time is exactly two days later, and I am riding down Mt Albert Road on the wooden seat my father has bolted to the handlebars of his pushbike so that he can pedal me about Auckland.

We stop at a capped stone wall. My father removes his bicycle clips, lifts me over the wall and we take a shortcut across a paddock of long grass, then we climb through a fence and we are in the grounds of the hospital. My brother doesn't look at all like the boy-companion my father has promised me, but appears to be instead a blind wrinkled red-faced doll. The mountainous belly has vanished, my mother seems to have slumped into her bed and the whole experience, so keenly anticipated, turns out to be a bit of a let-down. It's hard to know what all the excitement is about.

This is not to be my mother's last child, though at the time she swore it was. My half-sister Marion will be born almost ten years later.

But the important thing, so far as my parents are concerned in 1936, is that in just over five years they have produced four babies. There is a Labour government in power and there are plans to start a huge house-building programme. Times are hard, but it looks very much as though they are going to favour young married couples who are eager to go to bed early and copulate to populate.

My mother will march to the top of the queue when John A. Lee and the idealists of the Labour Party get cracking with their state-housing plans. She is breeding for the future of our nation. She is one of the healthy young optimists who plunge forward with their prams and pushchairs to fill the land with bonny bouncy babies. The downside of all that superfertility and spectacular childbearing is not revealed. I must live another forty years before my mother confesses the truth.

The corrected version of the story is appalling. My mother has since told me that she was driven off her head with childbearing. No precaution, except total abstinence, seemed able to keep sperm and ovum apart. Husband and wife only had to look at each other and another new life would be kicking at the lining of her womb. And there weren't just the four children. It was far worse than that. In those short five and a half years of manic reproduction, my mother confessed to me that she also fitted in a late miscarriage and a cheap backstreet abortion. This was followed by an operation for an enormous ovarian cyst. She nearly went mental. She felt as though she was condemned to a state of perpetual pregnancy and reproductive ailments.

Everything her mother had told her about the filthy-dirty nature of human coupling suddenly seemed to have come true. Sex was a nightmare.

9: A PIE & A CUP OF TEA

When my parents arrived back in Auckland from their world travels, and my father had lived out his dream of witnessing the Red Dawn in Moscow, my mother was pregnant again (with my sister Carole) and the family was almost, though not quite, destitute.

The only money my father had left was a single half-a-crown coin (twenty-five cents) in his pocket. Then two small events occurred to remind him that even if he may have been convinced that he had experienced a few moments of personal political euphoria, nothing had changed in the larger day-to-day world of practical human relations while he had been away.

When he signed off his ship in Auckland, the first person to speak to him was an out-of-work Londoner who touched him for the price of a feed. 'I'm as good as broke and I'd just come all the way back from England, and what's the first thing that happens?' my father said to me years later. 'A homey comes up and puts the bite on me.'

I reminded him that he had told me he had only one half-a-crown in the world, and asked what he did.

He explained that the whole situation struck him as being so bloody rich that he took the down-and-out into a café and bought him a pie and a cup of tea. 'What else could I do?' he said. 'As a general rule you never gave a beggar money for food in the Depression. He'd always sneak off and spend it on beer. So you always went in with him and pushed the cash across the counter yourself.'

The second incident was just as telling. One of his close relatives had become quite well off, in spite of the Depression, so later the same day my father looked him up and asked for a small loan to get started again. The answer was frosty. 'We'd all like to drop everything and have a good time gallivanting around the world, wouldn't we?' he was told. 'But some of us believe in standing by our businesses and our families. You've made your choice, so you'll just have to find your own solution to the difficulties you've made for yourself, won't you?'

It was an appalling knock-back for my father, who had always imagined he was extremely close to the other members of his family, and he deeply resented having no other option but to go back a second time and – as he later described it – 'beg for a loan that the bastard knew I'd bust myself repaying in double-quick time'.

The story offers an interesting glimpse into the rigid personal disciplines that had been necessary to triumph over the Depression – and how, in the tricky way of these things, disciplines can so easily assume the status of great virtues. My father and mother had behaved frivolously by 'gallivanting around the world' and now they had to go through a ridiculous process of ritual humiliation before being helped.

Yet below these surface proprieties and dissimulations, Anarchy was up to its everlasting capers. The oldest of the Jowsey boys was Frank, who was a hypocrite of the first water. A man of high principle and rectitude, a dedicated semi-fascist 'thinker' and an enthusiastic social climber, he dabbled in various business ventures which presented plenty of front but little substance, married unhappily, bred several children and one day discovered himself to be in more trouble of a personal nature than he could cope with, so he simply disappeared (to Australia as it turned out), abandoning his family without warning and without the price of their dinner or a penny in maintenance. It was his proud boast in secret communications to his brothers in New Zealand that he had a swish house on Sydney's North Shore, a flash MG motorcar and a voluptuous mistress, and that he was on the visiting list at Government House.

At my father's insistence, in 1959, I stayed for an uncomfortable few days with the awful Frank in his Sydney home. The only reason I didn't walk out after one night was because I was utterly compelled by the situation he and his partner lived in. I had never met people like them and it allowed me firsthand observation of a way of life that I would otherwise have had to guess at. I spied on them in fascination and without shame.

Never before had I been the house guest of uptight crazy-right-wing bourgeois citizens who lived 'in sin', as the relationship was often called at the time, and the bullshit morality was wonderful to listen to and to

UNDER THE BRIDGE & OVER THE MOON

note. Frank's woman lived up to my every expectation when she took me aside, after I'd been in the house for only a couple of hours, to make it clear that, despite all appearances to the contrary, I should understand that she was really a respectable businesswoman in her own right, with her own source of income. In no sense of the word was I to think of her as being 'kept'.

She was actually a kind and attractive person, who happened to be in a vulnerable position according to the laws and public values of the time, and her amusing bitchiness and hilarious pretence to style, glamour and impeccable standards of behaviour made up to some extent for Frank's vile humbug and contemptible snobberies. But when I finally packed my suitcase and left a day or two later I was glad never to visit the house again.

George, the third-oldest brother, was also a complete rogue, but he was as warm and easygoing in his attitudes as Frank was sanctimonious and miserable. As children we were all spellbound by George – until we lost sight of him when he pulled off a coup that suddenly made New Zealand too small for him. Like Frank, he too found it convenient to go into exile in Australia.

The story went that George owned a farm whose buildings he had managed to grossly overinsure. One night, when George and his wife were sitting in a picture theatre at Huntly, a flash came on the screen asking him to go to the box office. When he did so, he was told the bad news that the fire brigade had been called out to his farm. Of course, George and his wife rushed to their home, only to find that it had been burned to the ground.

However, George was always ready with a smile, a wink and an appropriate cliché. He could well afford to assert that 'Every cloud has a silver lining,' for he discovered that his loss was going to make him quite well off.

The insurance company that had accepted his valuation was naturally not very pleased and they put private investigators on his tail, but they couldn't pin any wrongdoing onto him and eventually they were forced to pay out. As George described it, in terms of mock outrage, one particularly nasty investigator actually had the bloody nerve to say to him one night that, though he may have thought he'd conned the company and got away with it, they would never forget him or give up on him. From now on they would be watching every move he made. They would never give him any peace. And one day he would inevitably make just one tiny little slip, and when he did they were going to nail him to the bloody wall . . .

They were as good as their word. The police and the insurance investigators made things so hot for him – so he would explain with a shake of his head and a puzzled grin – that he thought he'd take his doctor's advice and go to Australia for health reasons.

George was a compulsive big-stakes gambler, and my father once made him a lot of money when by the merest fluke he was staying with friends in Rotorua and saw his brother's name advertised in an Australian newspaper that was torn up and skewered on a nail banged into the dunny wall. George was listed among a roll-call of Tatt's minor prize-winners who had never claimed their money. My father sent away for a full list and found a heap of other prizes that George had never claimed. He used to buy tickets on Tatt's whenever he felt lucky, but he simply couldn't stand the tedium of checking out the minor prizes. He was owed hundreds.

The second-oldest brother, Harold, was the most like my father, who was the last born in the family. They used to visit each other often, and between the two of them they could have supplied the whole world with a convoluted consideration, and occasionally even a firm opinion, on every matter known to mankind, plus some.

Harold was a successful businessman, although he claimed that this didn't stop him from being able to 'see through the system', and he shared my father's faith in the Red Dawn. He was also a dogmatic health fanatic, with an absolute faith in compost, carrots, apple juice, yoghurt, lettuce, tomatoes, energetic mastication, fresh air, regular bowel movements and twice-baked bread. Unfortunately, for those who tried to dismiss him as a mere crank, he proved his theories and the power of his mind by surviving until he was eighty-seven, when following a stroke he refused food and willed himself to death.

Harold's Epsom house, with its long entrance drive skirting a tennis court, was one of my favourite places to visit when I was seven or eight years of age. It was a wonderland of illustrated books, where I could curl up on the floor all day, away from my brother and sisters, and spend my time in silence, fact and sublime fantasies. Harold's two sons, Victor and Keith, were quite a bit older than me, so they had not only outgrown a large part of their library (and their high-quality boyhood clothes) but also a magnificent Dinky-toy collection and a Meccano set, which I was also allowed to play with as a solo treat. I swear that I was so conscious

UNDER THE BRIDGE & OVER THE MOON

of this double honour during the war years, when there was an almost total lack of handsome books and quality toys, that I never left a smudge on a page or knocked a single chip of paint off a tin truck.

Harold's wife, Kathleen, shared the same name as my mother's third sister. She was the kindest and most gentle person I remember from my childhood. She was born in 1899 and, by dying at the age of ninety-six, only just failed to achieve the remarkable ambition of having been alive in three different centuries.

The brother who completed the Jowsey male line-up was my uncle Wilfred, who was nearly always referred to as just plain Bill. He was the second-youngest boy, and the only quiet, modest and genuinely humble personality in the family. He was a very good carpenter and cabinetmaker who once allowed himself to be talked into a business venture with my father, making tables and chairs. It didn't work out to be worth the effort and anxiety, and since he got a basinful of both at home, he gladly went back to a life of wages. He had two lovely daughters, but they hardly made up for the tribulations visited on him by his wife and her aptly named twin sister Mona. When Bill got married he found to his surprise that Mona moved in with them on a permanent basis, though the poor man was never consulted in the lifelong arrangement that the sisters planned for him. One day Bill had the compassion born of experience to warn my father (who was still single at the time) that it would be in his best interest to scram quickly and permanently, for the sisters were hatching a plan to marry him off to Mona.

My father told me that some people used to laugh at Bill behind his back, though there was nothing funny about him or his life. His brother was a good and even-tempered man, entirely without ambition. He was one of the best, and though his fate was an odd one, he met it with sly humour and when that wasn't enough he endured it in silence.

10: An astral satisfaction

My Aunt Eva was my father's only sister. The company of so many energetic, dogmatic and argumentative brothers (Bill apart) had no influence on her, except perhaps to drive her deeper into a lifetime's depression. She was a proper wet blanket, never sparking, never laughing. As children we used to swear we could smell her coming from miles away. From her heavy drab dresses and fox furs she gave off powerful gusts of dank mould and mysterious soupy smells.

Eva drifted around the country, from one poverty-stricken business venture to another, until she had the good luck to latch on to an ancient and decrepit couple (a brother and sister), who found her so lacking in speed, unpredictability, initiative, chatter, gaiety and glamour that she suited them ideally. She had arrived on their doorstep a bit like a stray dog, and they had had the good judgement to allow her to snuggle into their home and become their perfect devoted companion. At last, she had found a true mission in life.

When these two admirable people died, Eva inherited sufficient funds from their estate to smooth her own retirement into a nursing home, where she was watched over by the kindness of my younger sister Carole, who visited her at least every week, though how she managed to put up with our aunt's vague and maddening docility I've no idea. As for my brother and me, we never managed to change our attitude towards her. We could forgive and feel intensely sorry for her, but we never liked her, for we always felt that she had properly diddled us in a particularly mean-spirited adult-powerful way.

It all now seems harmless and a little sad, but as children it gave us a bitter sense of resentment. We had taken our bikes to Rotorua and had crossed the terrible road over the Kaimai Range to Tauranga, for a holiday at what was then the wilderness of Mount Maunganui. When we came to leave by train for Auckland, we obeyed our father's instruction and bought our tickets from the tiny travel agency that Eva owned on the Tauranga waterfront.

Dad had promised us that, because she was our aunt, she would share the profit she made off our tickets and we'd get them at a discount. Instead of which, she not only charged us full price for our fares, she whacked a shilling booking fee on top.

My brother and I argued the toss with her – for there was a whole shilling at stake, at a time when you could buy a bag of aniseed drops for a halfpenny – but she glared back grimly and told us not to be such miserable little twerps. She waved the tickets in our faces and said she had a living to make, and could we have imagined her travel business was some kind of public charity?

'Dad told us you'd give us a discount,' we grizzled. 'We've only got a shilling in the whole world.'

'Pay me the shilling, or you can get on your pushbikes and pedal all the way back to Auckland,' she told us. 'The tickets have been issued, so you can only get your money back by applying at the Auckland Railway Station. And you'll have to wait, and even then you won't collect all of it, because they'll deduct a repayment fee.'

The road back to Auckland was mostly metalled in those days, not quite as bad as the one we'd crossed from Rotorua, but a damned sight longer. And a shilling wasn't going to provision us. We knew we were beaten, so we handed over the money and spent the journey back home, penniless and almost sick with hate, discussing the various ways we'd like to see our aunt put to death.

When we complained to our father about the way she'd dealt with us, he was furious, and when he next saw her he tackled her about the way she'd robbed her own relatives. But Auntie Eva was unrepentant. As far as she was concerned, she was a travel agent, she supplied railway tickets at a cost-plus fee (despite the fact that her tiny ticket booth was no more than a minute or two from the station), we were her brother's sons, and since he was better off than she was, she was entitled to share his good fortune.

It is easy now to see that there was a rough justice in her attitude, but that wasn't apparent to my brother and me at the time, because the way we looked at it, the money hadn't been given to us by anyone; we'd worked for it ourselves and we'd been swindled pure and simple. What we had no insight into was Eva's hand-to-mouth poverty and the way she could never have seen us as her nephews, but as a pair of young larrikins waltzing up to her counter, laughing and skylarking, with a rattle of silver in their pockets. She would have been hungry and she would have been looking directly at her dinner. Who could have blamed her?

Before she was adopted by her kindly brother-and-sister rescuers, then looked after by Carole, I had one other startling intersection with my aunt. I must have been about eighteen or nineteen, and I was sampling all the religions around Auckland, to try to discover what they were on about and to see if they had satisfactory answers to the Great Abstract Questions that bothered me at the time.

My quest meant that I checked out a lot of very mad people, for to my astonishment wherever I searched I found religious nutters all over town. There were hundreds of them. Some may have seemed pretty harmless, but there were more than a few who were seriously disturbed, among them several frothing puce-faced tambourine rattlers and spirit raisers, all with small congregations of glassy-eyed devotees who, from the evidence of the enormous broods of infants attached to their congregations, looked as though they had decided personally to populate the planet with true believers.

One night, at a well-attended meeting of the Theosophist Society at the top of Queen Street, I heard a remarkable lecture by a visiting Englishman. At first sight he seemed the average, small, roly-poly, elderly man in a dark suit whom you'd pass every day in the street, but his voice was unforgettable. It was fruity yet passionate, a bit as though he'd left his tongue out in the sun and it had gone juicy and overripe. The words that issued from him were almost squashy.

The man told us that we were very lucky people indeed because he'd just been told by an international statesman whom he was sworn not to identify that we would all shortly be saved by four wise men from Tibet, who had managed secretly to smuggle themselves into the 'four corners' of the world, from whence they would create an intense electrical force by beaming their spiritual energies along an astral plane which would wipe out Atheism and Communism forever and at last allow his listeners to enter a higher state, which naturally he himself had already attained.

It was a very enjoyable performance, given by a man who was obviously quite doolally, but who found that no impediment to getting by comfortably as a public speaker with a bold line in flat-Earth specialities. But, as if all that wasn't entertainment enough, when I got up to go I almost bumped into Aunt Eva. I was amazed to see that she and a few of her friends wore gorgeous aprons, covered with symbols, some of which appeared rather like Egyptian hieroglyphs and others more like astrological signs from Old Moore's Almanac. As fancy dress goes, Eva's get-up was a knockout, and for the first time in her life she seemed pleased to see me.

'I see, Kevin, that you have at last come to me in search of astral truth,' she smirked.

I've always been glad that I managed to keep a straight face. Just as in retrospect I'm delighted to think that Eva found a path to cosmic consciousness and got some higher and larger satisfaction out of life. When I think of that little travel agency in the cubicle on the waterfront at Tauranga I can only believe it was owed to her.

11 : THE DEATH MACHINE

Although the writings of such Theosophical luminaries as Madame Blavatsky may now seem little short of dippy, and though some of her claims to supernatural experience were exposed as fraudulent, the broader spiritual movement that she represented, together with such magnificently absurd characters as Annie Besant and Edward Carpenter, paved the way for two major achievements.

The first was merely unlikely. This apparently waffly movement actually brought together a powerful lobby that encouraged the formation of a Society of Authors in England, to protect and promote the interests of authors (and publishers) through such campaigns as the introduction of an international agreement on copyright. But by comparison, the second achievement seems not just unlikely but bizarre.

The movement that led to meetings such as the batty one in Queen Street, where I saw my Aunt Eva in full regalia, also happened to inspire the Irish poet William Butler Yeats, who was to write some of the finest (as well as some of the silliest) poetry of the twentieth century. He deservedly picked up the Nobel Prize for literature in 1924. So, what should one say, when confronted by that little item of evidence, except that the Golden Dawn must have had something going for it?

I raise the question only because there is an absurd latter-day footnote to it. During my Theosophical investigations I discovered that the elderly English lecturer who had brought news of the four Tibetans who would save the world was by no means alone in his lunacy. Several people I spoke to were possessed by a wistful millennarianism that seemed to reflect the flip side of a general spirit of doom. It is easy now to forget that at the time we all lived under the terrible threat of an atomic war between the USSR and the USA, and the consequent likelihood of the end of life on Earth.

The most memorable of these fervent pessimists was a young man I met in the Society's library. He was pretty ordinary-looking for a crank – sportscoat, neatly creased trousers, sober tie, short-back-and-sides haircut – so I was surprised when he confided in me that he was working on an invention to save the world. It was a machine that would harness the limitless resources of universal psychic energy through an arrangement of wires, crystals, switches, valves and condensers and, although its construction was involving him night and day in a desperate race against time, he had almost perfected it.

When I asked what he hoped to do with the machine, he gave me a perfectly bland smile and announced, 'When I pull the lever, my machine will instantly wipe out all the Communists everywhere on Earth.'

'Wipe out all the Communists?' I repeated. 'The whole lot?'

'Stone dead.'

'Come again?' I asked. 'Do you mean the card-carrying ones?'

'Oh no,' he said blithely. 'My machine will investigate people's minds, classify them all and kill everyone with subversive thoughts.'

'Phew, that could mean executing a lot of people just for thinking,' I pointed out.

'It'll obliterate the swine in their millions,' he agreed proudly. 'All of them. Totally erased. Gone for good.'

'And who'll be left?' I asked.

'Theosophists, spiritualists and freedom lovers,' he said.

12: FIRST LOVE

Spinsterhood is an interesting and useful term that seems almost to have fallen out of use these days. Originally, a spinster was an occupational description only: as the word indicates, it referred to a person whose job or habitual activity was to spin wool, linen or cotton.

Spinsters could be of either sex, though because they worked at home they were more likely to be women. Eventually the term became associated with women of marital age who for one reason or another were obliged to remain at home; it was then adopted as a legal term for women who were unmarried, though it often had an extended meaning: women whose prospects of ever finding a husband were reckoned to be just about zero.

It was this association with undesirability that has made the 'spinsterish' condition sound so unattractive to modern women. There

UNDER THE BRIDGE & OVER THE MOON

has come to be something pinched, forced and miserable about being a spinster. Unlike the word bachelor, there's nothing jolly or carefree about it. The best a young unmarried woman could hope for not so long ago would have been to be described as 'a bachelor girl' – meaning that she *chose* to live a single and independent life away from home – but the current aversion on the part of most young women to being described in male terms, let alone as any kind of 'girl', has rather told against that. Yet my Irish aunts, Moya, Biddy (Kathleen) and Sheila were proud of their spinsterhood. They had worked at it. I once saw my aunt Biddy fill in an official form and enter, under the heading 'marital status', the word 'spinster'.

After I had asked her what marital status meant, I enquired what a spinster was. 'It means I'm my own boss,' Biddy said with unmistakable self-satisfaction. She clearly felt power and independence, and nothing demeaning, about describing herself by that term.

Because my mother was busy running a *family* household while actively pursuing her own intellectual and political interests and ambitions around town, besides sharing out sporadic and selective attention to the four children she had given birth to with such concentrated energy, I found myself increasingly shunted off to stay in Biddy's home in Douglas Road, Epsom. And here was a domestic set-up entirely organised and presided over by a spinster.

Of all my aunts, Biddy was the most dynamic. When Mac, her father, became widowed, she provided him with a roof over his head for years, and her sisters Sheila and Moya moved in with her as well when they stayed or lived in Auckland. She was a brilliant manager and her home was entirely different to ours. There were no toys scattered about the place, no smell of bodies, no piles of washing and ironing. Everything was neat and polished. It was an adult household and I was expected to be a kind of junior grown-up in it. The rules were a lot less casual than those that applied in houses with children in them.

At Douglas Road I soon discovered that my Aunt Biddy's two other unmarried sisters also described themselves as spinsters. Sheila was far younger than Biddy and Moya – in fact, she would often joke that she was an 'afterthought', a word that I could never quite work out – and since she joined the airforce as a meteorologist early in the war, before eventually becoming a schoolteacher, I saw her only very occasionally. It was Biddy and Moya who shared me between them and lavished their time on me – and it was Moya who first conquered my heart.

The curious thing is that both at the time and later my sisters and brother thought Moya cold, bitter and sharp-tongued. They merely hated Biddy, but they loathed Moya with an uncompromising ferocity. Yet I discovered her to be one of the most lovely, tender and good women I have ever met. She was intensely shy and stammered in front of adults, but in the company of young children she became confident and fluent, and as with her three sisters, the school inspectors awarded her the highest grading marks achieved by any teachers in the country.

It was Moya who taught me the magic art of placing my right-hand forefinger on the fat letters of a primer and tracing the squiggles of our alphabet, until I could remember them by touch and sight then piece them together into pronounceable words.

She would take me aside and spend hours sitting next to me, guiding my hand across the pages of books and instructing me how to unlock their secrets. I could feel her body trembling as she held me close, speaking softly, with her hot breath tickling my ear, willing me to excel at reading. I glowed with the pleasure of our intimacy. Under her instruction, not long after my fourth birthday, I could read every book that she taught her primer classes at school. No wonder my siblings detested her. Who could blame them for being jealous? I was her chosen one. We were really and truly in love.

Nearly twenty years later, I was sent a message, through my mother, that Moya was in poor health and would like to see me one evening, if I was interested and had the time. It was a typically diffident Moya-style invitation, but it was accompanied by a private warning from my mother that Moya would be much changed. Of course, I found the prospect of seeing her irresistible. Yet as soon as she opened the door I wished I hadn't gone.

Moya had given up being a strange superbly talented spinster and had decided, too late to think of having children of her own, to get married. Her husband would possibly have been a nice-enough sort of bloke left to his own carefully ritualised life of work and a few beers, for this furnished him with some vague appearance of normality and stability, but his effect on Moya was disastrous.

As soon as she saw me, Moya staggered over the threshold of the door and clutched my shoulders for support. I grabbed her and stopped her from falling over. The dress she wore was stained and torn. Her breath was sour with what smelt like a mixture of booze and vomit.

'My little K-K-Keggy boy,' she stammered. 'You c-c-came to see me as soon as I c-c-called . . .'

Then she looked at herself and began to weep. 'Look at me,' she added. 'I'm just an old and ugly d-d-drunk. What in C-C-Christ's name h-h-happened to me?'

Her husband appeared and helped get my aunt inside. 'So you're the bright spark she keeps talking about, are you?' he asked belligerently, when we'd got her into a chair, where her head hung over to one side and a dark sticky liquid began to foam at the lower corner of her mouth. 'Well, I'm bloody pleased to set eyes on you at last and see you're not up to all that much after all. Would you like a beer?'

I said I would and asked him if he didn't think he should call a doctor.

'She's like this every night,' he said. 'It's the jungle juice. It's got her in the legs. The quack says he's going to have to amputate one of them.'

We had a beer and after a while Moya opened her eyes and began to stammer and slobber over and over again what a good little boy I'd been, keen to learn and always polite and never answering back, and how the little boys of today were a pack of nasty bastards and you couldn't trust any of them.

'See what I mean?' her husband griped. 'You've always been the apple of her eye. And the rest of us only give her the pip.'

I finished my beer and left and never saw Moya again. I had forgotten till that time that she had been the first woman, apart from my mother, whom I'd ever really loved, and that she too had loved me. It had been the real thing.

It is not stretching the meaning of the word to talk about the 'love' between a four-year-old boy and his thirty-something-year-old aunt. Everything I have ever learnt in life persuades me that love is the strangest sensation we ever encounter. It may arrive in many strange misshapen forms but its memory remains with perfect clarity. True love transforms our existences and it is the single experience we never forget, no matter whether it becomes mangled in the heart or whether we try to deform or suppress its signature in the mind. Moya was one of several women I remembered when I wrote these lines:

> on the spring day
> that love was born
> the wind whipped
> the budding thorn

on the winter's day
that love was dead
the thorn ripped
and the wind bled

It is a young man's poem, full of a young man's awareness, but I have
only to glance at the words again to realise with an itch of discomfort
how I'd played the little angel to Moya with my whole being, because
that was the role that her love had demanded from me. When I wrote
that poem in my mid twenties it was an attempt to project myself into
the larger drama of love and the nostalgia that follows it inevitably,
partly, I suppose, because it embarrassed me to think that I hadn't always
managed to sustain my 'shrimp with attitude' image. Love had the power
to turn me into a proper little sonk after all. No young man of my
generation would ever have enjoyed having to face up to that kind of
discovery.

When I now replay key memories of my life from the private
projection room of my mind, I often try to rearrange the picture and
imagine what would have happened if I'd had the wit, the gumption or
the common sense to have done this or that, instead of some of the
dickhead choices I made; but there is no alternative memory for Moya.
The thorn did rip and the wind did bleed, though these are metaphors
for something else, something both more universal and abstract.

My one last true memory of Moya is more particular and more
squalid than the way the poem puts it. The scene always ends one
winter's evening in drunken misery, with her frothing at the mouth and
babbling on about what a good little boy I'd been, and with my first
true love about to lose a leg, then die.

13: TORMENTING THE FLESH

Before such errands became not just 'incorrect' but downright illegal,
it was one of the highlights of the week to be sent from Douglas
Road, up Ruapehu Street to the corner of Balmoral Road to fetch

UNDER THE BRIDGE & OVER THE MOON

Mac the weekly indulgence of his threepenny cigar. I would have three huge copper pennies or a shiny threepenny-bit placed carefully in the palm of my hand, asked to recite the precise instruction I would give the tobacconist, then finally my fingers would be folded tight and I would be reminded of the colossal value of the coins I was being entrusted with.

No bribe of sweets or icecreams was ever necessary; the joy of holding such a huge sum of money and being sent on such an important mission was its own reward. My chest would nearly burst with the excitement of the responsibility I had been given and the service I was about to perform. And when I got to the tobacconist's the man behind the counter would listen to the instructions I recited, examine the money carefully, then select a box from a shelf behind him, lift the lid and let me choose which of the identical cigars would most please my grandfather.

I loved the ritual and pretence of it all, and the whole delirious process always took some time, because I would stand there and breathe in the perfumed wonder of the box and examine at length the chubby big-breasted young ladies in long dresses whose pictures adorned the lid – until the man behind the counter would at last say that if I didn't choose soon my grandfather would be sending out a search party, and I would select a cigar and race back with it to watch the elaborate ceremony of the light-up take place and the first volcanic plume of heavy smoke vent into the sky over Douglas Road. After which it would be my 'job' – and supreme honour – to blow out the match.

Mac had installed himself at the back of Biddy's home, where he kept a ferocious black brute of a tomcat – a snarling monster that would leap over his arms and roll on its back with its feet in the air, but only for its owner. It wouldn't let anyone else come near, and it only answered to a loud whistle. Mac explained to me that his cat thought it was really a dog and he had used it to round up the cattle back on the farm – and I believed him. Besides this terrible animal Mac was able to salvage only two other vastly different but equally prized possessions from his wipe-out in the Depression: his tools and his books.

Along the walls of his room he would store his Kelly axes and his shovels and spades – all made from the best steel and looked after as affectionately as if they'd been shiny sporting trophies – and on makeshift shelves, beside and between the tools, he stacked hundreds of books, mostly poetry or pink-bound Left Book Club volumes published in the 1930s by Victor Gollancz.

The whole backyard at Douglas Road became a lush vegetable garden, as the three public interests of my grandfather's life now became reduced to politics, poetry and pottering about the garden. There turned out to be another secret interest, but I wasn't to learn about that for another forty years, though perhaps I might have guessed at it from his habit of rising every morning at six, summer and winter, and tormenting his flesh with a cold bath.

This cleansing operation was always followed by a healthy breakfast, then Mac would labour for a few hours at his plants before the sun was too high in the sky and only a fool would dig or hoe beneath it.

It was his unfailing ritual each evening to soak a bowl of prunes and a pot of porridge for the household breakfast. It was a great privilege to be woken by Mac and to be allowed to stand next to the warmth of the coal range and stir the porridge, which had to be cooked to a perfect smooth consistency with no trace of burning. Mac had a simple unswerving faith in prunes and porridge first thing in the morning, not just for the high-energy goodness they provided but as a means of purging and purifying his bowels.

Bowel-consciousness was one of the great obsessions of the first half of the twentieth century and was far more widespread and more vigorously practised than is now generally acknowledged. The memory of its formal rites and the fearsome instruments of torture by enema still terrify me so much that I've never forgotten the spectre of the enamel receptacles, the dull brown hose and the fearsome black nozzle with its tiny tap.

The prize text of the movement (if that's not an unfortunate word) was a book called *The Culture of the Abdomen*, written by a stool-obsessed fetishist called F. A. Hornibrook, whose sketched image graced the cover in a stylised attitude, complete with imperious glare, impressive handlebar moustache, muscular torso, tight trousers appropriate to his interests and a not-too-successfully-concealed compulsively disordered personality.

Once, when we were living in Pete Avenue, near Royal Oak, my younger sister and brother stole Mac's prunes while he was taking a late afternoon nap. Mac's rage at having the order of his life upset was like that of a maddened elephant. I just happened to be an amused bystander, but that made no difference. With surprisingly nimble speed he picked all three of us up in one hand by our scrags, like a bunch of kicking yowling pups, and plunged our heads under a garden tap, one by one. I have faced many varied and vicious punishments in later years but none was more horrific than that.

UNDER THE BRIDGE & OVER THE MOON

And the secret interest? Well, of course it was the last thing grandchildren ever suspect in the aged heads of their family. It was sex. Mac was a ferocious puritan. From my earliest years he was always warning me of the dangers of drink and loose women.

Drink was the demon of the family. It had killed his father and would carry off his daughter Moya. And he claimed to have been a regular drunk himself until, at the age of twenty-four, in Australia, he and the shearing gang he had worked with had spent their season's cheque in an outback pub, then been kicked out in the street when the money was gone, without the grace of a last pint or even a bite to eat. The callous indifference of the publican horrified as well as enraged him. He and his mates went back and wrecked the pub, but there and then Mac swore off booze for life, and although he would go into pubs with those who invited him he would always hit the sarsaparilla, and he never touched another drop of what he referred to contemptuously as 'shypoo' so long as he lived.

Mac was an all or nothing man, so it was the same with sex. His wife had loathed the act of reproduction, and after she had borne him four daughters, plus the two sons they had had to bury, she considered she'd done enough to further God's plans and there were to be no more disgusting carryings-on. So he found that a cold bath every morning was one way of sublimating the troubles that his dreams still visited upon him.

The procedure worked until he was almost seventy. But while he was staying with Biddy in a country town, he got talking one day to this young lady of twenty-six – for as I have already indicated he was a brilliant talker – and somehow or another they ended up making secret assignations. I don't know many of the details, but the next thing there was a scandal and the young woman had a child by him.

My mother has told me that she has a half-sister out there somewhere, whom she has never met. Over the decades I often asked for the name of the woman involved, but she steadfastly refused to repeat it to me, on the grounds that there is too strong a likelihood that it would do no one anything but harm – and especially the unmarried mother and her child.

I would always take a chance on that. But families, when they wish to bury the truth, do so resolutely inside themselves and there is no way, short of chance discovery or hiring a team of private investigators (and perhaps not even then), to find where the evidence may be. Families are not just kindred groupings, they are secret societies, and their deepest secrets are concealed from each other.

14: THE MAN IN THE BOX

When my father and mother returned from overseas, we moved along Mt Albert Road to Pete Avenue, near Royal Oak. My younger sister Carole and my brother Anthony (who was always called Mit, an abbreviated child-speak corruption of 'Mister') appeared in the next two and a half years and almost immediately began to grow alarmingly larger than me.

In fact, Mit was a monster. At the age of two he was like the young Hercules and, egged on by his three older and far more crafty siblings, he launched himself with gusto and good humour into a childhood of bravado, minor crime and mayhem.

As a toddler Mit was obsessed by anything that gurgled. Drains, pipes and taps held an irresistible attraction for him, and our indoor lavatory, with its rumbling, cascading flush toilet, gave him endless rapturous delight. In the 1930s there were still outside dunnies in many suburbs of Auckland, some with weekly nightsoil collections, and indoor lavatories were only just beginning to replace them, so our Pete Avenue house was right up to the minute. However, since ancient customs take some time to die, no one used our modern facility in the dark, for everyone still kept their own little chamberpot under their bed, just as nearly everyone had done for countless generations past.

Mit discovered a great opportunity in this old-fashioned arrangement. He would be first up, and ignoring the discomfort of his wringing-wet nappies, he would make straight for the marital chamberpot which glowed with its amber glories of the night from beneath our parents' bed. He would seize hold of the pot, and with precocious determination and strength, he would stagger with it to the lavatory and tip its contents down the bowl, then bring the gleaming trophy back triumphantly like an Olympic athlete.

One morning, however, my father and mother managed to almost fill the pot to the brim and the effort of emptying their efforts proved beyond even my brother's superhuman strength. He lifted the pot above the lavatory bowl, lost control and with a fearsome detonation and a roar of fluid like a tidal wave smashed both to smithereens. Only a butt of shattered porcelain, like the broken stump of a giant tooth, still stood fixed to the floor. The mess spilled halfway through the house.

If that was the most spectacular visual memory from our days at Pete Avenue there were others of more lasting impact. The most decisive event – or so I thought – was my father's election to the Three Kings Primary School committee. I pleaded with him to use his influence to obtain special permission for me to start school at the age of four and a half, though it was a local doctor whose enthusiasm (and signature on the necessary form) actually worked the trick.

It was a huge mistake. Moya had taught me to read up to Standard One level, so I was in a fever of excitement when I walked through the gates at Three Kings at the beginning of the school year in 1938. Here was my chance at last to immerse myself in writing. The secrets of our language would be unlocked and I would enter the grown-up world of signs where all mysteries would be made clear.

That first day was the most miserable of my life. I hadn't been in the place five minutes before a hulking boy with staring eyes marched up to me and asked if I'd like a sock. Innocently I pointed out that I had socks of my own.

'Well, how would you a sock from me?' he asked so angrily that I thought perhaps I'd please him by saying yes. It seemed the best policy, since I was a year younger than most of the other children and a runt into the bargain. To my astonishment the boy then gave me a tremendous punch that knocked me over.

I went straight to the teacher and reported there was a dangerous boy among us. The teacher was trying to keep the peace by hammering the piano keys louder than the blubbering, bawling and brawling infants she was in charge of and she yelled, what made me suppose he was dangerous? 'He's just given me a sock,' I explained, using the word in the new definition I'd just had revealed to me.

'A sock? A sock?' she screamed. 'What kind of language is that? Come back again when you've learnt to speak properly. We don't use words like sock at Three Kings.'

Here was a world quite unlike home. It was without order, justice and comprehension. It was a world full of unreliable meaning and uncertain authority. No one made sense. It was a world in which you could get punched just for trying to be agreeable. On my first day of formal education I discovered a terrible truth that I would never forget and which would protect me for the next twelve years: school was a madhouse, ruled by experts in petty nonsense and policed by bullies whose laws were based on absurdity, whim and contradiction.

And worse than that, it was a place of desperate disillusion. All I wanted to do was learn, but what happened? We sat around and sang infantile songs and drew pictures of 'Our House' on small sections of the narrow blackboard that ran around the back and sides of the classroom.

Our House had to be built like a box, with a door in the middle and a window on each side of it. The walls had to be white and the roof red. Above the house there had to be a fluffy white cloud from behind which a smiling sun spread out its rays like the spokes of a golden bicycle wheel. In front of the house there had to be a lawn and a path, and a very silly-looking flower. On the path stood your father and mother – exactly as they never stood in real life. Day after day we learnt how to complete the details necessary to exactly portray this suburban ideal. We were children of a compulsory and perfect dream.

And there was worse to come. We were told to raise our hands to ask questions, so I lifted mine to ask when we could start on the Standard One Reader. The teacher almost choked. 'This is the Tiny Tots class,' she said. 'No one is able to read in Tiny Tots.'

After several weeks of repetitious and ludicrous struggle our class managed collectively to wade far enough into the alphabet to chant over and over again 'c-a-t spells cat, d-o-g spells dog', while the teacher rhythmically thumped a pointer on the sheets of paper that displayed a cat and a dog with lettering underneath.

I can remember to this day weeping with despair, then drifting off into a dream-world that was full of unauthorised and unconventional conjunctions. It was a place of silent fantasy where the cats and dogs spelt interesting words like Persian and Pekinese, and where the houses could be any damned shape or colour you pleased, and your parents could get on with digging the garden or washing the nappies, and the front paths could float off into the skies and drift through the clouds if they wanted to.

However, I shut up and said nothing about this. Three things looked pretty near certain. One: if I asked another question the teacher would only get mad at me again. Two: if I tried to be polite some thug would make it his business to offer me another sock. And three: no logical explanation would ever be given for all this bad temper, stupidity and savagery. It was my first experience of a world without reason.

If I had been cleverer and more practised in mysteries, I suppose I may have picked up a vital clue to the infinite contradictions and curiosities that control our lives from an earlier and richly instructive appointment with 'the man in the box'.

I grew up when electric noise machines, which could be turned on and off with a switch and which needed no dexterity or talent to play, entered homes for the first time in human history. Children now grow up in an environment of lights, sounds, images and devices that operate by invisible forces, and they consequently accept them as an expected part of their everyday environment. But anyone who recalls the first impact of a wireless set more than sixty years ago will find it easy to understand how primitive societies have been totally overwhelmed by the sudden impact of western technology.

My father sat me between the handlebars of his pushbike and pedalled me around to the Kelly household, where my mother's cousins Percy and Hughie lived under the absolute sway of their sparrow-sized mother – this in spite of the fact that both men were prizefighters, as well as waterside workers. Percy later became famous as the only man to cause an industrial stoppage over a New Zealand sporting event when an American referee gave a verdict against him in a fight in the Auckland town hall. The fight was an elimination contest for a crack at the world title and the crowd judged that Percy had won. Next day the whole Auckland waterfront closed down and demonstrators marched up Queen Street to town to demand (in vain) a rematch with a neutral referee.

The Kellys were always the most courteous of men and there were the usual formalities while we sat around and drank tea and discussed at length the wellbeing and immediate prospects of the family and all its extensions. However, I could sense that something was up, for there was an unusual excitement in the air and Percy and Hughie kept glancing at a huge shiny box in the corner of the dining room.

Finally, after much nudging and winking between the men, Percy led me over to this box and told me that my father had secretly built it himself as a surprise for the family and I was to have the honour of turning it on. The box was at least twice my height and it was beautifully veneered. In its centre was a small moon-shaped metal aperture with a dial and beneath it were three large knobs. Below these lay a large and ornately fretted circle, behind which was fixed a piece of yellow-and-black patterned material.

'Twist the knob on the left,' I was told.

I did and immediately the metal aperture lit up with a dull golden glow. Behind it there came a strange humming and crackling sound.

'It's warming up,' someone explained. 'Just wait and don't touch the other controls.'

I waited, then to my astonishment a man's voice came from inside the box. I can remember walking straight around to its back and peering in. For all its huge size, the box contained only a single tray of wires, metal fittings, faintly glowing glassware and, below this, a large round apparatus that I later discovered was called a loudspeaker. Otherwise the box was empty.

'What are you looking for?' my uncle Percy asked.

'I'm looking for the man in the box,' I replied.

Percy, Hughie, Mrs Kelly and my father slapped each other on the back and laughed and wiped tears from their eyes. Over and over again they kept on saying, 'He's looking for the man in the box.' And each time they said it they'd start laughing all over again.

Percy and Hughie eventually fetched a friend with a small truck to transport the huge apparatus to Pete Avenue and they brought the joke with them. For years afterwards people in the street would ask if I'd found the man in the box yet, and at home the wireless was often referred to as the man-in-the-box machine.

At the time I hoped that if I pretended to take no notice all memory of the joke would fade away. Yet the picture remains with me as if it all took place yesterday. I remember the day precisely, the ride on my father's bike, the pea-green matchlined walls of the Kelly kitchen and dining room, the words that were said – but most of all I remember my stunned amazement when I looked inside the back of the machine and found no one there.

I flatter myself that I have an excellent memory, but over the past twenty years or so I have been constantly reminded by friends and family of events they insist were of great significance in our lives and relationships, yet I often can't place myself in the time, place or company that they are talking about. I have forgotten, or perhaps buried or contrived to suppress, so much that has occurred over the years that huge hunks of my life no longer exist. My head is full of memories that I wish to cling to and none I can't bear to live with. I walk around to

UNDER THE BRIDGE & OVER THE MOON

the back of the experiences and peer in and find nothing unexpected.

The difference is that I am no longer shocked at not finding old presences. I'm glad to stare in and find that nothing haunts me, that there are no ghosts. The man in the box has given up on me at last.

15: 'I, A STRANGER AND AFRAID . . .'

My last decisive memory of Pete Avenue is of the paddock that also served as the airfield at Royal Oak. I am four years old and my father and I are watching the ungainly Tiger Moths bump and wobble across the grass as they taxi to take off. They pass only a few metres away from where my father holds me on the top of a fence so that I can wave to the wizards in leather helmets and glinting goggles who peer over the rims of their cockpits then rev their engines and roar up into the sky, where the forces of the air instantly transform their machines into magic instruments of winged beauty.

Then one of the Tiger Moths stops alongside us and the pilot shouts to my father to carry me over the fence and lift me into the cockpit and he'll take me up for a ride. I ask my father if he'll come too. Room for one only, the pilot says.

Then I'm not going, I say.

My father tells me not to be a bloody fool.

But I have just been given a terrifying lecture by my mother on never talking to strangers and never-never-ever accepting rides with them anywhere or under any circumstances. Obviously the man in the Tiger Moth is a stranger. The merest glance at his helmet and goggles confirms it. Besides, he wants to take me for a ride. So why does my father not understand the peril he is trying to place me in? My mother has told me that strangers are very bad men and they take little boys away and never return them, and terrible things happen to them and sometimes they never see their mothers and fathers again.

I grab my father around the neck and scream at him to take me home. Then I turn and see the pilot laughing at me. My father also laughs, but he is embarrassed. His son has turned out to be a proper little sonk.

In front of the family that evening he tells my mother and elder sister about how I nearly had a ride in an aeroplane. He is still embarrassed and he is also horrified, not at my narrow escape from a stranger, but at the waste of a priceless possibility of unique adventure. I had been offered the chance of winging through the clouds. Perhaps, no matter how long I lived, I would never have the same opportunity again.

At about my age, just before his family packed up to come to New Zealand, my father had seen Blériot's flying machine on Scarborough Sands. After soaring all the way across the English Channel, it had been carried, pulled and pushed the whole length of England so that the entire population could share the wonder of a contraption that could travel more than twenty miles through the air without having to land. And in the thirty-odd years since Blériot's feat, he has never managed to come nearer an aeroplane than that, and he has never himself dreamed of stepping into one and actually flying. Yet here I am at the age of four turning down a miraculous opportunity as though I could ever expect to have the same good luck again. He says that he will never understand how a son of his could be so profligate and stubborn.

I yell that I have nearly been taken for a ride by a stranger, and my father and mother and sister burst out laughing.

The world of words gets crazier every day. It turns out that I am not to believe that a man dressed in a peculiar rig-out, whom I have never met before, and who invites me to hop in his aeroplane and come for a spin through the sky, is not to be classed among the category of men known as 'strangers'. He is a generous and well-intentioned man, and the next time he asks me to take off with him I am to go – although I may as well get used to the disappointment of having almost certainly passed up my only chance ever to fly.

Yet it is not the irony of having since travelled many hundreds of thousands of kilometres by air or having used aeroplanes as my father used trains that nags at my memory. It is the thought that in a couple of years these same pilots who are bumping their flimsy machines across the grass at Royal Oak will be flying the wartime skies over Britain. These ex-strangers will be the heroes of the fantasies of every small boy in the land.

UNDER THE BRIDGE & OVER THE MOON

16: GRIMM DIGS

Pete Avenue was the Inner Kingdom of my earliest memories. I was vaguely aware of other places such as Whangamomona and Queen Street, Auckland, but Pete Avenue was the huge hub around which a very small world revolved, mostly in silence and darkness.

Then it all changed. One day in 1938 Joe May, who was in the carrying business and was a friend of my uncle Harold, arrived with what he called a 'lorry', because it was a huge and enclosed vehicle, and not to be confused with a mere open truck. Joe loaded all our possessions into it and off we set to the far-off Outer Kingdom of the North Shore.

The journey turned out to be all of four or five kilometres across Auckland and included the thrill of an ocean voyage – a ten-minute trip by vehicular ferry across the Waitemata Harbour, from Mechanics Bay to Devonport.

Then we were introduced to the glory of our new home. Because of my parents' uncontrollable fecundity we had been given one of the first of the Labour government's brand-new state houses in Devonport. It was box-like, solid brick, but it was spotless, shining and perfect. There was a washing machine, with its own electric wringer, in the laundry. Narrow Neck beach was a minute or two's walk down the road.

The whole area was like a park. In fact, the old Devonport racecourse was just around the corner, and though it was kept in neat order it was no longer used for race meetings. Only a few years before our arrival it had been declared too dangerous for jockeys and horses. It has since become the Waitemata Golf Club.

You couldn't even see the gasworks, which stood where there are now soccer grounds, but with only a little effort you could gaze on the beauties of the green volcanic cones of Mount Victoria, North Head and Rangitoto, or look out to sea and watch the yachts and scows and great passenger ships coming and going just offshore.

My mother was happy. She had now left behind the last associations of the Depression and she had been transported to a paradise on Earth. Everything that had been promised by the dreams of her father and the great reformers of the Labour Party had come true.

Or so it seemed – for a few months at least. This was a time I think back on as the golden age. How else to express it but in the brilliant shimmer of memories of the ordinary and the everyday?

It is an indisputable fact that mothers
are endowed with sensory perception, thought

and wisdom sacred to their vocation.
This threefold power is never taught,

it comes with the whole package and
passeth all understanding. It defies analysis.

Mothers can undo magic spells, love
beyond reason and cure with a kiss.

My mother even knew when I was raiding
the biscuit tin. 'It's easy,' she said.

'All mums are born with a hidden eye,
and mine's in the back of my head.'

Well, if that was how it was in our new house, it wasn't destined to last. I remember the day it ended, the day I heard the first quarrel between my mother and father. Their voices were angry, and between their accusations, which seemed to be concerned with something called a 'bungalow' and the number 'six hundred', but which I couldn't understand, they kept telling each other to pipe down or the children would hear. I couldn't believe what was happening. To hear my parents snarling at each other like this was against nature. It was terrifying. It was a disfigurement of all existence.

Then my sister Ann put her arm around me and explained that Mum and Dad were having an argument because we were moving house again. We were leaving our beautiful new brick home and we were going to live in a dirty old shack that Dad insisted was a bungalow. He had bought it for a bargain six hundred pounds and it was in Rewhiti Avenue, which was in the middle of Takapuna, three kilometres north along Lake Road.

My mother explained decades later that, with hindsight, this was the breaking point in the marriage. My father had no understanding of what it was like to be perpetually pregnant, then to be given a clean start in a new house, only to have it taken away again and be forced to return to the old life of squalor and inconvenience. Nothing could ever be the same again after what she considered to be her husband's wilful selfish act of betrayal.

I also shared a feeling of despair. I had enrolled at the beautiful little Vauxhall School and I was in my element. Unlike the appalling

UNDER THE BRIDGE & OVER THE MOON

experience of my first day at Three Kings, here the teachers encouraged me to dip into any damned thing I liked and helped me with difficult words. They believed in freedom, advancement and the joys of learning. For them, school was the open door to a world of discovery. And on top of everything there was the marvellous infant mistress whom I shall thank and honour all my life for throwing us into the deep end of literature to experience total immersion of the imagination by reading to us daily from the Grimm brothers.

Not a thing was smarmied over or concealed, in the way the teaching loopies of today take it on themselves to 'protect' our children's imaginations by distrusting and debasing them. We got the truth about Hansel and Gretel, and what they really did to the wicked witch. And nothing was spared in the telling of the frightful lessons of Rumpelstiltskin and the Three Billy Goats Gruff. It was like being led into a cave and shown how to locate and open the treasure chest of the mind. The whole accumulated folk-wealth of our culture was made available to us. It was scary, brilliant, shattering and enriching beyond our dreams. This was what I had come to school to learn.

Then it was back to 'c-a-t spells cat' and 'd-o-g spells dog' at Takapuna Primary School. I stood up and for a dare spelled 'T-a-k-a-p-u-n-a spells Takapuna' for Primer Two and got myself shifted to Primer Four where I was told by the Infant Mistress that I was to sit still with my arms folded and not to let out a peep, for I was a naughty boy for trying to look too clever and if I did it again I'd be sent to Old Pop Matthews, our headmaster, who would give me 'six of the best' for the trouble I was causing.

Once again it was the same story: sit tight, dream away and try to remember to keep your trap shut. It seemed to be the only way to avoid the attentions of some grown-up monster, straight from the Grimm brothers, who for no fathomable reason would seize you by the arm and belabour the palms of your hands with a length of cowhide till they swelled so red and purple that you couldn't grip a knife and fork when you got home and were called to eat your tea.

But after a few initial violent shocks, my first year at Takapuna actually got much better as it went on. I may have been young, but I wasn't completely silly and eventually I decided that even if it would never be a patch on Vauxhall, life at Takapuna simply had to be a bloody sight better than getting a sock at Three Kings.

17: A WORLD AT WAR

The 'bungalow' we moved to in Takapuna was exactly as Ann had said. Compared with our gleaming state house, it was a shack. We were back to a wood-range, an outside dunny, rotten floorboards, water-stained ceilings, dingy floral wallpaper sagging from its backing of scrim and sarking, borer-infested matchlining covered in dark scummy varnish that got under your fingernails, doors and windows that stuck or rattled in the breeze and the overpowering stench of decades of mildew, tobacco and boiled cabbage. Every crack and corner was heaving with black bugs, slaters and silverfish.

But, my God, how my father worked. He was off on his pushbike selling insurance by day, then just about every evening and weekend, when he wasn't called out to talk some poor vulnerable family man into gambling a sixpence-a-week stake against the long odds of his dying, he'd be straight into the house, knocking down walls and ceilings, and digging out the old totara foundations and repiling the house on concrete blocks.

The range was ripped out first, and it offered an unforgettable foretaste of the chaos that was to follow over the next twelve months and more. As my father gave the cast-iron structure a final wrench with the crowbar, which sent it slewing a metre or so across the floor on a set of rollers, it brought down a section of the ceiling with a deluge of soot and dust that hit the floor then exploded through the whole house. We were blackened. The filth choked us, though somehow my mother managed a scream that filled us with horror.

For a year we lived like a family in transit to a destination unknown. Walls would come and go, floors would be raised and lowered, a new roof rose over us, a fireplace with an outside chimney appeared on one side, an electric stove was wheeled into the kitchen, built-in cupboards and wardrobes were fitted into every room, we even got a bath with a real shower – all while we shifted from room to room as if we were camping out. But my father was a marvellous tradesman and one day – or so it seemed in the spectacular foreshortening of my child's mind – I woke to find I was living in an entirely redesigned and superbly rebuilt bourgeois Takapuna home, complete with attached garage which housed our tiny convertible Austin Seven.

How my father managed to accomplish so much work in just over a year I've no idea, and how he arranged the finances on his insurance agent's fees and commissions is even more of a mystery. However, my mother gave me a clue long afterwards that could point to an explanation. She claimed that she was forced to scrape by on an allowance of exactly half-a-crown a day with which to feed and clothe the whole family. The coin was placed in her hand in the morning, and although she was an intelligent well-educated mother of four in her thirties, she was never trusted with the whole week's seventeen shillings and sixpence in one lump sum.

We are dealing with people who had just been through the Depression, so the story may well be true, although I have to say that it doesn't tie in with my own memories of a father whom I found to be generous, at least in his later years. However, in those early days in Takapuna we certainly lived frugally. We ate sloppy scrag-end stews or meals of boiled threepenny-mince and onion, supplemented with a lot of free fish from the sea just down the road, plus occasional buckets of pipis that we collected at low tide from the beach, and we bought vegetables direct for pennies from the Chinese market-gardeners who farmed land that ran down to Shoal Bay. Desserts were always boiled fruit and custard, penny jellies or rice, tapioca, semolina or sago pudding.

In addition, we soon had a fowlyard full of productive White Leghorns and Black Orpingtons (they *had* to be productive or they smartly sacrificed their lives to the pot). But it took some time for us to establish the large and bountiful vegetable garden we developed in our own backyard, for the soil initially was a heavy yellow clay. However, the whole family toiled hard on it. After easterly storms we would all go down to the beach and wheel up barrowloads of seaweed to fill the long deep trenches my father had dug. And – these were the days before large-scale looting was made possible by sophisticated greed and modern technology – we would bring up bags of sand to make the soil more friable.

My father had a sense of purpose and achievement. He was providing for his family in a prime position in the one area he had always loved since he was a small boy in Freeman's Bay and used to take the ferry over to the North Shore to lie on Takapuna beach – and where he had won a medal for swimming to Rangitoto and back, a total distance that was well over ten kilometres, allowing for the tides. He was proud. This was something that responsible heads of households set themselves to accomplish. But in the course of doing all this he had made my mother angry and unhappy.

And suddenly the whole world was at war, and so far as the Jowseys were concerned it was on two fronts. A domestic battle-in-miniature had broken out inside our home at Rewhiti Avenue, and outside we were gradually made aware of a conflagration that was spreading around the globe.

In the summer of 1939–40 both wars were at what was called an early, 'phoney' stage. But they were real enough to us. We were soon going to learn new meanings to fit our vocabularies – new definitions for familiar words such as pillbox, front, trench, spitfire and zero – and we would acquire words that had previously had no application or relevance in our lives – words such as separation and divorce.

As children we did not have either the experience or the vocabulary to make exact distinctions between these wars. They were much the same to us. We were simply apprehensive and perplexed. Yet inwardly the unnameable pressures left their marks. Mine were to become expressed by regularly and inexplicably pissing my bed. It did not become a habit for some time, but in a manner of speaking it could be described as an emotional reaction which began as a mere trickle of helpless bewilderment that eventually turned into a full-scale flood of confusion.

My father and mother pleaded with me and wanted to know what was wrong. But there was nothing they didn't know better than I did. There was no grammar and vocabulary that I could use to explain something I couldn't identify. What was I supposed to say? 'I'm pissing myself because the way things are going, this family is heading towards disaster'?

My brother and sisters laughed at my wilful refusal to control my bladder, but eventually my father stopped reasoning with me and lost his temper. After a few beatings I was threatened that I'd have my nose rubbed in my sheets if I didn't stop.

And that's what happened. I got upended over and over again and suffered a child's version of keel-hauling. Of course, all it did was make me even more obstinate in my pathetically infantile attention-grabbing displays and it cured nothing. If anything the appalling punishment actually made matters worse. It nearly always does with stubborn children.

18: A POISONED CHALICE

The signs of domestic disaster at Rewhiti Avenue were obscure at first, for there were also moments of delirious happiness. For instance, I have total recall of one sublime summer's day in 1940. My mother and father are working outside in the garden and singing a 'Little Birdie' song to each other, the refrain of which goes, 'Tweet, tweet.' It's the kind of grown-up baby language, with lots of kisses, that children love to watch and listen to.

Suddenly Dad wipes the sweat off his brow and says, how about cracking a bottle of beer; and Mum says she'd rather have a shandy thanks. Then Dad promptly fetches a bottle of beer from a crate in the garage and he counts a few pennies from his pocket and sends me up to the dairy at the top of Park Road to buy a bottle of lemonade.

I race on the wind. The errand is unprecedented. Never before has lemonade been brought into the house, for Dad is opposed to 'gut-rot' shop-sweets of any kind. When I get back Dad produces two glasses and I watch him fascinated as he pours out a foaming mixture of beer and lemonade. Then to my astonishment he asks if I'd like to finish off the lemonade bottle.

Would I like some of my father's and mother's loving lemonade? The question has to be crazy. I would die to be given a drop and I feel as though I would sing 'Tweet, tweet' forever in heaven. So I am sent to fetch another glass and the last of the precious fluid is poured out. Then, before I can stop him, my father adds a small portion of beer.

He may as well have offered me a poisoned chalice and been done with it. The beer is gut-wrenchingly disgusting. It makes the lemonade undrinkable. I gag and spit and rage with disappointment, but my father merely laughs and tells me to hand over the glass. He raises it with a flourish and tosses it down his throat in one long swallow, then wipes his mouth with relish.

The whole day has been washed out. But, if only I could have a way of knowing it, it is a foretaste of worse to come.

Meanwhile, the other war, the one that would be called World War Two and would kill tens of millions, was entering our consciousness and conversations through the wireless, the newspapers and the weekly newsreels at the picture theatres. For years there had actually been a terrible war raging in China, close at hand, but which we knew hardly anything about, for our attention was almost totally focused on raids and skirmishes that affected Britain – which everyone referred to as 'home' or 'the mother country' – and the European battle zone. Yet the war was brought home to us literally by a significant change in male clothing. Over the course of 1939 and 1940 nearly all the younger single men and a good many of the married ones began to strut about in uniform. Several local larrikins were gazed at with respect by the citizens of Takapuna for the first time in their lives.

A friend of mine had an older brother who joined the crew of the cruiser HMNZS *Leander,* so that instantly put me on first-name terms with a hero – even if my friend and I were to be bitterly disappointed that 'we' did not take part with HMNZS *Achilles* in ending the career of the German pocket-battleship *Graf Spee* in the Battle of the River Plate in 1939. However, 'we' did manage to serve with conspicuous honour on escort duty for troops sent to the Middle East and actually sank an Italian raider in 1941, though when, a couple of years later in the Pacific, *Leander* was torpedoed and badly damaged, with the loss of twenty-eight lives, my friend and I did not talk about the tragedy. It didn't fit our heroic understanding of how the barbaric enemy hordes were less than human and therefore incapable of getting the better of us. Besides which, by this stage of the war the navy had lost some of its age-old glamour to the air force.

Our allegiance to *Leander* became extremely wobbly after the Peter the Pilot campaign was supported by the Self Help grocery chain. You collected so many coloured cards from special packets of porridge oats, then when you'd filled a whole album, you sent them away and got a shiny Peter the Pilot badge. Boys who sported one of those on their proud chests could not have won higher esteem and envy from their classmates if they'd arrived at school wearing golden haloes and announced they were the Lord's anointed.

It was all part of the unreal and often absurd atmosphere of war that we gradually became accustomed to, until it began to seem like the natural order of life. Clothing, petrol and basic items of the New Zealand diet, like meat, sugar and butter, became rationed, though compared with what people put up with in other countries there was still plenty to eat. Rationing was never much more than a nuisance, and it even allowed the State to practise its new 'welfare' role of guiding us forcibly in our own best interests. A diet that reduced our intake of fats and sweets, and which encouraged the production and consumption of fresh fruit and vegetables, had to be good for us whether we liked it or not.

My father became an ARP (air-raid precautions) warden, walking around the streets at night in a steel helmet with a gas mask hanging around his neck, enforcing the total blackout. He had ignominiously failed his army medical examination, for he had ghastly bunches of varicose veins on the calves of his legs which rendered him incapable of marching, but worse than that his eyesight had been permanently impaired as a child by a double attack of scarlet fever and measles, and he was as good as blind without powerful specs.

The odd thing is that as a very young man during World War One he somehow wangled his way into the Territorials, and tried to get over to the Western Front. He made it as far as a call-up to Trentham camp, but was frustrated in his attempt to sacrifice his life by the lucky outbreak of peace late in 1918.

His official army photograph is a splendid tribute to youth and illusion. In 1918 there were not only army bands, but full-scale army orchestras. My father lies on the ground among a hundred or so recruits in their lemon-squeezer hats and puttees, all striking wonderfully arrogant poses, yet none of them is bearing a rifle. They present themselves for their future confrontation with Kaiser Bill and his ruthless Huns with musical instruments. My father is preparing to repel the beastly German rapists with his viola.

If that sounds ludicrous, it was nothing to the lunacy that we were subjected to and conditioned in as kids in the early years of World War Two. As a writer I've always felt extremely lucky to have witnessed public displays of sheer madness that would never have been allowed to develop publicly in the ordinary run of things.

When Japan simultaneously attacked Malaya and Pearl Harbor three weeks before Christmas 1941, we had already been through nearly a year and a half of war-conditioning. But suddenly the mood changed. The front line was no longer the Atlantic Ocean and the sands of North Africa. It was just to the north, in our own backyards.

As a nine year old, in 1942, I lived through one of the oddest experiences in our nation's history – an experience that adults now seem to have great difficulty referring to with truth and clarity. 1942 was the Year of the Japanese, and for about a dozen weeks, after the fall of Singapore and as the Japanese front line advanced down the Pacific towards us – until it reached New Guinea, Timor and the Solomon

Islands – there was a special, almost tangible intensity and stillness to all our lives. People seemed always to be huddled around their radios, waiting for news, and everything else seemed hushed. It was like waiting for the crisis in a fever to see whether the patient would pull through or not. One more victory to the Japanese, I heard someone say, and we were goners.

Then what seemed like a miracle happened. In May 1942, a large Japanese fleet on its way to take Port Moresby was intercepted by the American navy in what came to be called the Battle of the Coral Sea. The Japanese were turned back in a prototype modern-style naval engagement in which neither fleet saw an enemy ship, for each attack was made by carrier-based aeroplanes. The Americans suffered the loss of one of their large carriers, but scored a strategic triumph, a blow against Japanese military prestige. Victory at Midway and Guadalcanal followed. We were saved.

The curious thing was the way our cockiness returned immediately. We were on top again. We did not talk about the weeks we had hunched in silence over our radio sets. We forgot our terror. The 'Japs' were now going to be licked because they were cowardly, cruel, uncivilised and inferior. It was asserted everywhere that as a people they were capable only of imitation; they had no powers of invention. Soon they would be put back in their places forever.

In Coldicutt's Four Square Store and in the Self Help at the Takapuna shopping centre, which was never called that but always referred to as 'Hall's Corner', the dear old ladies of the district would mutter that the Oriental devils should be boiled in oil and exterminated. However, at school our teachers explained patiently that we were merely up against 'evil little yellow people' who were definitely not subhuman, though they gave every appearance of being so. Movies showed the Japanese to be incompetent, malevolent freaks of unsurpassable stupidity. In our schoolboy war games we preferred to shoot imaginary Germans; the Japanese were too far beneath our contempt.

But I think now that our arrogance was in direct proportion to the depth of fear from which we had just been delivered by the Americans. There was no doubt that we had all been in shock. People with relatives in the country had made arrangements to leave the cities. Some of the children in our street had already been packed off – as I was soon to be, though for reasons unconnected with the threat of invasion. A local priest told my father in front of me, at the bowser in the forecourt of the old bus barns, that he would 'personally see to it when the Japs get here, you're the first person in Takapuna put up against a wall and shot', and with this little slip of the tongue made it appear as though he had plans for collaboration – as my father was quick to point out when he offered furiously to take the lunatic around the corner to the Takapuna Police Station to have him turned in as an enemy agent.

People were off their heads with fear, though you'd be hard put nowadays to find anyone to admit it, or even think deeply about it.

19: ENTANGLEMENTS

The lighter side of the Year of the Japanese didn't seem funny during the worst weeks of the invasion scare, but it didn't take long for at least some – including the children – to realise that we'd all gone more than slightly mad.

Who would ever forget the day that an assortment of soldiers and civilians arrived on Takapuna beach, with hundreds of rolls of barbed wire and great stacks of wooden stakes? In no time at all there was a formidable system of entanglements running right along the beach at the high-tide mark. There were also five or six concrete pillboxes with gun-slits to allow rifles and Bren guns to cover the whole length of the sea front. Every so often a defile was left, presumably to allow concentrated fire, but more conveniently from our point of view, they made it possible for us to get through the barbed wire to go for a swim.

How these entanglements could ever have impeded a full-scale amphibious invasion was never explained. They ran only from the coastal defence battery at North Head to Milford beach – perhaps five or six kilometres in all. The long stretches of rocks were entirely undefended, as were most of the other thousands of kilometres of the New Zealand coastline. Those living in the seaside suburbs of Auckland city had been offered a visual palliative. They could look at the barbed wire and know that someone was doing something to make them feel safer. The whole thing could only have been done to raise civilian morale, for its practical value was nil.

Our schoolboy gangs took over the concrete pillboxes along Takapuna beach as soon as the Home Guard deserted them, and we used to squint through the gun slits and joke about the way even the Japanese would have had the brains to land on a nice long beach up the coast, such as Orewa or Waiwera, where there was no barbed wire and only a token force to confront them. After all, they'd managed to work that one out when they took Singapore.

We also used to fall about laughing at the way that, if the Japanese had really been mad enough to land on Takapuna beach, it would have taken them all day to form in ranks, answer a rollcall and pump up the tyres of their pushbikes, and by the time they got themselves organised to pedal down to the Devonport wharf they would probably have found they'd missed the last ferry. And that meant they would have had to hang about looking silly, whistling, with their hands in their pockets, while they waited an hour for the first night launch to get them over to town, one platoon at a time.

It was all too ludicrous; but there was worse. At Takapuna Primary School we took part in one of the most hilarious rituals ever devised to activate a small child's innate disposition to anarchy. Every child had to come to school equipped with a pair of earmuffs to shield their eardrums from bomb blast, and carrying a rubber eraser to bite on and protect their teeth from banging together and splintering. We practised what to do in an emergency, as air-raid shelters were quickly dug for us on a far playing field, but these turned out to offer enough room only for the infant classes, so the older children were told simply to run across Killarney Street and hide themselves in the long grass of an empty section. Of course, these sessions always ended in yelling, giggling and teasing, and girls and boys rolling about together, practising a thrilling variety of unarmed combat.

Because any fool could see that the school couldn't cope, it was hoped that there'd be sufficiently long warning of a raid to allow all the children to disperse in an orderly fashion to the imaginary safety of their homes, where every backyard had its own little shelter, dug into the garden and covered with a rounded sheet of corrugated iron.

This dispersal was to be signalled by a special ringing of the school bell, when we would all line up – not by class, in the ordinary way, but by street. The first trial was one of the greatest displays of adult-organised chaos that I've ever witnessed. The plan was for Old Pop Matthews to blow a whistle and the Hauraki Road and Minnehaha Avenue kids, who lived near the extremes of south and north respectively, would set off in a howling pack, followed street by street by the rest of us. 'Farthest first, nearest last' was the order.

But children never follow perfect plans like that. The whole thing developed into a riot, with the last trying to catch up with the first and with gangs trying to head off the smaller and weaker children and make them run for the mudflats or the beach. There were tiny children wandering the streets of Takapuna, lost, bewildered and bawling, and hordes of little gangsters dashing through hedges and leaping fences, throwing stones and insults at each other (the roads were metalled in those days, apart from a concrete strip covering two thirds of the width of Lake Road). It was one of the great shambles of the century and if the Japanese had decided to bomb us that day, God only knows what worse could have happened.

The outcome was that we went back to the old system. The infants had the air-raid shelters and the rest of us went back to rolling about, having fun in the long grass.

The adults were more serious in their madness. Practical manifestations of this came in two main forms: the crazy little backyard air-raid shelters that inevitably filled with water in the first downpours of autumn, and the broom cupboards where buckets of sand were kept for those cool-headed citizens of Auckland – who somehow happened not to be sitting waist-deep in water inside their shelters – to sprinkle over incendiary bombs when they came crashing through their roofs.

There were also posters identifying the silhouettes of friendly and enemy aircraft – presumably because it was important to know the correct name of the bomber that was raining hellfire on your head.

Some sensible pamphlets were also distributed, urging everyone to put aside a box of tinned food and first aid supplies, not to offer themselves as easy targets to strafing planes (presumably by performing such reckless acts as standing outside in the street trying to identify attacking aircraft from their silhouettes) and above all not to panic.

But some of the authors of these pamphlets found a wonderful opportunity to offer lunatic information and bizarre advice. The grandly named Coromandel Emergency Precautions Service, confusing the dangers faced by the sparse populations of Colville and Coroglen with memories of the hazards of life in the trenches of the Somme in World War One, issued preposterous instructions on the hospitalisation of the wounded and the identification and different treatments for attack by chlorine, phosgene, mustard and lewisite gas.

The Whangarei Borough Council issued a notice to mothers which amounted to a preposterous demand that none of them should lay down their brooms and run, for 'if Whangarei is raided or attacked, you must stay where you are, just as a soldier has to'.

And the Onehunga Borough Council came out with a masterpiece of madness that talked to its ratepayers about how morale should never be allowed to flag, for 'no bombardment can stop messages from God coming through' and, with a flourish of superb triviality, recommended everyone have writing materials handy so that, while they were being attacked, they would be able to write these messages down as the Almighty delivered them.

Frank Sargeson once told me that he had tried to puncture some of these foolish fantasies and one day, when things looked their grimmest, the poet R.A.K. Mason called on him and said that if the Japanese landed New Zealanders would fight them on the beaches, fight them – well, if necessary, in the bush, the mountains, the fiords, and so on.

Frank asked him if that meant that everyone would be expected to live off the land – and quite probably poison themselves on fern roots. Ron Mason got hot under the collar and maintained that, in spite of the difficulties, all New Zealanders should join the patriotic resistance.

At which point Frank elaborated a nonsense scheme of his own, based on the knowledge that, contrary to our own war propaganda, the Japanese did actually have a bit of civilisation – after all, didn't they make quite a feature of their tea drinking? Surely the best thing to do, he said, was to go down to the beach as the landing craft came in, swing the billy and offer the invaders a nice cup of tea. No milk, of course.

It has always seemed to me that although Frank's plan may not have worked, it certainly had an improved sense of intelligent improvisation. It has also seemed to me that perhaps Old Pop Matthews should have abandoned all those absurd dashes into the long grass, where we secretly practised wrestling with the girls, and spent his time teaching us the finer points of the Japanese tea ceremony.

20: A SEVERED BED

L ooking back, I can now trace the course of the disaster that hit our home, but at the time everything happened so gradually over two or three years that nothing very much appeared to be wrong. In fact, although it has from time to time seemed to me extraordinary that two people could share a bed with such sustained sexual intimacy that they would breed four children yet fail to realise their incompatibility, the real surprise of my parents' marriage is that it took so long to fall apart. Like so many people who were reckless enough to call themselves radicals or progressives in those days of depressing public subservience, they were expert at defining the world's woes and amateurs at defining their own.

The irony is that my parents' ambitions were the exact reverse of the conventional expectations of the 1940s. My father was a domestic animal. Home, children, carpentry, garden, selling insurance and a spot of fishing, with left-wing politics for excitement, were quite enough for him. But my mother had gone to university (until hard times put a stop to that) and to training college, and the domestic routines, which she happened to be skilled at, bored her silly. She longed for a life of books, 'free thought' and brilliant friendships. She was a good-looking bluestocking born in a sullen age of slump and war, brought up on a backblocks farm, then cast into circumstances that made her intellectual energy and ambition seem arrogant and destructive.

The sign that something terrible had been happening was as decisive as it was absurd. I arrived home one day to find the parental bedroom in chaos. The sheets and blankets were stacked up, the mattress had been dragged outside and my father was sawing the bed frame into two halves.

'Why are you sawing up the bed?' I asked.

'Ask your mother,' my father answered. His face was almost crimson with exertion and fury.

So I went to my mother and put the question again. 'I can't sleep properly,' she explained. 'I need my own bed, just like you.'

I can remember crying. What would now happen to all those marvellous mornings when I had crawled into the sweet yeasty warmth of the double bed and snuggled against my parents' flesh? A world of absolute certainty and miraculous pleasure was being abolished. It was as though the wicked witch from *Snow White and the Seven Dwarfs* had walked in and cursed us. But there was worse to come. My parents had begun to acknowledge that they were living separate lives.

The fact is that my sisters and brothers had known and accepted for some time that something was up, even if they didn't talk about it much, but I absolutely refused to acknowledge it to myself – and I had the advantage of being able to shut myself off entirely and bury my nose in my books. I could never allow myself to admit a connection between pissing my bed and what might be happening between my parents, because I didn't have the words to do so – and only words made things explicable and therefore 'real'. Besides which, I had attained a special condition of privilege that I was desperate to preserve.

My mother had been going out a lot at weekends and in the evenings, and from the age of about six or seven I had been allotted the special distinction of accompanying her. Among the groups she joined was the Rationalist Association in Symonds Street, and when she was elected onto the committee I became a regular attendee at her meetings. When she made speeches on women's rights, secular education and the future of religion, or debated the existence of God with all who would dare do battle with her, I would be sure to be there in the audience, soaking up every inflection of her speech and adoring her.

As someone who had been educated by nuns (whom she never ceased to thank and admire) my mother was especially fond of putting Jesuits to the sword, and though I found many of the words a long way over my head, I thrilled to her performance as, radiant with sincerity, she tormented her opponents with argument and scorn.

I also tagged along with my mother and became a regular visitor at John A. Lee's house in Grey Lynn after he was thrown out of the Labour Party. My mother became a fervent follower of his cause and eventually stood for Parliament in the Otahuhu electorate as a Democratic Labour Party candidate in the 1943 general election. None of Lee's supporters was successful, and Lee himself lost his seat, but my mother told me long afterwards that my father and she were separating at the time and one of his accusations against her was that not only had she been having it off with several of the males in the Rationalist Association, but that she'd become John A. Lee's lover.

She agreed that she had been invited to bed many times – as any handsome and spirited woman, moving in circles that described themselves as 'progressive' 'leftist' and 'free-thinking' might expect to be

– but denied that she'd ever accepted more than once when she was actually married. Which hardly seems likely, but may just be true – as if anyone could now be any the wiser by knowing or caring.

What I do feel, however, is that I was made use of as a 'cover' for assignations and this earned me special and utterly undeserved consideration when the inevitable split occurred. All that I had been turned into was a trusting, precocious little simpleton, and I still feel guilty for being the one child to be sent away to be looked after by Mac and my aunt Biddy while my siblings were condemned to go through the worst hell of the break-up.

Biddy had reached a salary bar as a teacher and had to do country service, so shortly after she and Mac left Auckland to fulfil this requirement I was sent away from home to join them.

I remember being taken to Auckland Railway Station, given a ticket and put on a train to Frankton Junction, where I had to change to the Cambridge train. It was an easy enough thing for a city boy to do, but as a precaution – and ritual humiliation – my mother stitched a cardboard identification to the lapel of my coat, stating my name, home address, destination and reason for travel. Then, for the umpteenth time, I was made to recite a whole set of travelling instructions. And finally my mother spoke to the guard and to everyone sitting around me to tell them my name and to ask them to keep an eye on me and make sure I made the Cambridge connection.

I waved goodbye and got out a book. But while I read, my hand went up to the identification tag and slowly pulled out the stitches. Then I crumpled it up and hid it in a pocket. I was damned if I'd be labelled by anyone – I was ME, and would be so long as I lived.

Of course, I wasn't to know that no one can hope to move around the world without passports, identification papers and name tags of various kinds, but I've always felt a 'label' was different from a mere document of convenience. The memory of that train trip and the hateful label on my lapel, and the feeling of being dispatched into the distance without choice, like a parcel in the post, remains with me forever. And the sly subversive flush of happiness as I removed my cardboard consignment note was my first ever blow for personal freedom.

21 : A TASTE OF SOPHISTICATION

The Takapuna I temporarily left behind at the age of nine was just beginning to be overrun. If 1942 was the fearful Year of the Japanese, then there was no denying that 1943 had to be the brave new Year of the Yanks. They were our allies, but their arrival changed the way we were. Nothing would ever be the same again. They were outrageous and utterly marvellous.

The first Yanks we met actually appeared in 1942, in small numbers and for short stays, before being sent up to the Islands to try to stem the remorseless advance of the Japanese, and there was nothing very unusual about them, apart from their accents. They wore hats rather like the lemon-squeezers worn by our own troops. They were tough, modest and self-contained, in the same way that we considered our soldiers to be, and they didn't make much of a show, for they were career soldiers and they were here to do their job. Many of them had to be billeted around Auckland, for there was only limited room in the army camps.

I remember them coming to our house and how reserved and polite they were, always calling my mother 'Ma'am' and my father 'Sir', even when one lot proceeded to drink themselves unconscious in our sun-porch. Word had got around that my father could supply them with cheap fortified plonk from the Henderson vineyards, and that was what they seemed to need most in the brief time they had left to them before they sailed north to fight – and with good reason, I've always thought. They were good professional soldiers, the best in their army, and a high proportion of them were being sent to their graves.

Because of our crazy liquor laws, a highly illegal but intricately organised home-retailing system, called 'sly-grogging', had grown up throughout the country and my father's garage was used for a few months as part of this socially useful do-it-yourself distribution network. The secret of its success was that the supplies were acquired and passed along quickly and discreetly, so as not to attract attention from the neighbouring wowsers who pried on their districts vigilantly and venomously from behind the camouflage of their lace curtains. But having these unfailingly well-behaved soldiers coming into our home to sample the goods soon became too unnerving as well as being too obviously risky.

The group who got pissed in our sunporch had just received their embarkation orders, so they sat around in a little circle together, cleaning the rifles they took with them everywhere, and passing around whole bottles from which they drank with stolid glugging determination. They did not joke or laugh, but every now and again one of them would make short muttered statements about the 'Mighty fine firewater you make in these parts, sir,' then he would keel over almost sedately. They all ended up AWOL, but I hope their officers made allowance for that. As far as my father was concerned, however, their presence was far too noticeable and it meant real trouble. His venture into the liquor trade had to be terminated abruptly. The dozens of cartons of sly-grog were carted away one night shortly afterwards to someone else's garage.

The Yanks who followed these hard, impressive men, were a different breed. They were the youth of the industrial wastelands of the Depression years – mere boys, most of whom had never had jobs. They had been taken out of their no-hope backstreets and sent off on their travels to save the world, but first they had been scrubbed and trimmed, fed three meals a day, dressed up in smart gabardines and they were provided with wads of magical dollars in their pockets – not to mention endless sticks of Dick Tracy chewing gum and Hershey bars, and packets of prophylactics.

These young men were streetwise and brash certainly, but they were utterly good-natured and they put no value on their wealth other than the good time it could provide. There was almost no such thing as a mean Yank; they were sublimely generous. When they spoke, it was with words and accents that seemed to echo all the way from Hollywood, and they had a relaxed and almost careless glamour. All the children loved them. They had none of the aggressive reticence and gawkiness of young New Zealand men. The Yanks seemed to us to be easygoing big kids themselves and when they set off on route marches, from the army camp around the back of Lake Pupuke, where the North Shore hospital now stands, we would be there whenever we could to march behind them for mile after mile, swinging our arms, singing their songs and saluting them whenever they stopped for a breather.

We called our activity 'cadging', for that was our entire purpose in attaching ourselves so shamelessly to the US Army. We were like shoaling piranhas, waiting to strip the infantry of every cent, every bar of chocolate and packet of chewing-gum they were worth. We were a rabble of unscrupulous, devious little mercenaries, ready to race into dairies to buy them icecreams and soft drinks to slake their thirsts – and to accept the inevitable invitation they gave us to 'Keep the change, buddy.'

It was awful; it was a disgrace. But nothing our fathers and mothers or Old Pop Matthews himself could do would stop us. We became Hershey bar junkies. We'd think of that delicious chocolate, so sweet and creamy and sophisticated compared with the wrapperless penny Santé bars we were used to, and a compulsion would come over us and off we'd sneak again to join the marchers.

But the prize pickings for children were actually to be had from the monster army dump the Americans piled up at Barry's Point. It was a dangerous, poisonous place and we were strictly forbidden to go anywhere near it, but legends of the wealth to be mined from it were so attractive that every now and again we'd risk a beating at school or home, or a kick in the arse from the guards or the Takapuna police, to pick over the huge rat-infested mountains of rubbish.

For New Zealanders, who in those days never threw away anything that could be used again, it was like a kind of inside-out Aladdin's Cave. At home we used to save and sell or recycle bottles, tins, papers, boxes, rags, lengths of wood, bags, assorted bits of metal, rubber bands and pieces of string. All these things had domestic and sometimes commercial value, and every house had drawers and cupboards, or a shed or space beneath the floorboards, where these precious items were kept. But the Americans to our mixed horror and delight, simply chucked them away and dumped them, often unsoiled and unused.

One day word got around that for some mysterious reason Barry's Point had been left completely unguarded. Hundreds of boys arrived running or on bicycles from miles away. The place swarmed with them. Soon there wasn't even room for a blowfly. With our bare hands we tore into the mounds of treasure, screaming and squabbling as prize after prize was uncovered. We ate ourselves sick on what we were thrilled to describe as 'perfectly good rubbish' that the profligate Americans couldn't be bothered to open and had slung away intact.

Whether or not anyone died of ptomaine or blood-poisoning I've no idea. There were dark whisperings that some did, but as boys we explained the risks away by repeating what the adults always told us – 'There's a bloody war on, isn't there? So what else would you bloody expect?'

It was useful to be able to save grown-up simplicities and store them away at the back of your mind. Just like the bottles, tins, papers and

UNDER THE BRIDGE & OVER THE MOON

rags we never threw away, a stack of clichés took up little space and you never knew when they'd come in handy.

22: Country matters

My aunt Biddy had sole charge of a one-roomed school tucked away in an isolated valley at the back of Cambridge. The school was the sole focus for a farming community, which was connected by a metalled road that looped through a valley for about a dozen kilometres. Besides its educational function, the school also served as a social centre for a monthly dance and a monthly church meeting, which were held on alternate fortnights. There was no village as such, and there were no shops; just the tiny school, the schoolhouse and the outlying farms.

Next only to my short experience of the miraculous little Vauxhall School in Devonport, my stay at the country school run by Biddy was the happiest of my life. It was exactly the kind of place I imagined schools to be when I was very little and begged my father to let me enrol.

There was hardly any sense of competition, for the total roll varied between nine and a dozen, exploding temporarily to sixteen when an extremely fertile sharemilking couple turned up for a season with nine children and babies in tow.

Biddy was a resourceful and enthusiastic teacher, and she managed to keep the whole classroom hard at work and interested. Farmers' sons and daughters who had been treated as dummies by previous teachers suddenly began to shine.

Even the three illiterate glum and brutalised children who rode six kilometres from their remote farm to school, then all the way back again in the afternoon, began to read and write. These children were the victims of a rural destitution that many New Zealanders did not know existed, for it was a destitution that resulted not just from a lack of capital, poor land, hopeless methods and low-quality stock – though all of these were factors – but from a whole poverty-stricken culture of casual cruelty, pinchgut misery and wilful neglect. It was a poverty of the spirit as well as of the pocket.

The family lived in a shack, but the only thing that made this disgraceful was that no attempt was made to straighten the place up and make simple achievable improvements. The rundown pernicious inferiority of the farm had entered the souls of those who worked it and they seemed hellbent on seeing that their children caught the infection. It was said right around the district that each day began with screams as the children were flogged from their beds at four o'clock to bring in the cows for milking. Hand-stripping was the order of each day, to get the last drop of cream from the withered udders. Then a breakfast of tea and bread and dripping was followed by the long ride to school, with sacks for a saddle on the one lame horse all three were forced to share.

Mac had lived through that kind of treatment, so there was never a day when he did not get to school early, to make sure that there would be a large mug of cocoa for every child as he or she arrived. In winter he would also fire up the big potbellied stove in the single classroom so that every child would associate warmth and pleasure with a place of learning. He would also have handkerchiefs for the three who had come farthest, so they could blow their noses, and he would always have something for them to eat. When they inevitably nodded off over their desks in mid morning, Biddy would always let them sleep in peace and never allow the other children to jeer or snigger.

Biddy was an inflexible frosty old-maidish woman, entirely without the secret softness I had discovered in Moya, yet these children managed to locate some sort of honest and upright kindness in her. It must have been a vast improvement on the vicious drudgery they could expect at home. Occasionally, when they thought that other children weren't around, they used to clutch hold of her and sob their hearts out, not over anything in particular, but just because they had found some reassuring source of human stability where they felt it was safe to open their hearts.

I witnessed this ritual twice, unobserved, and on both occasions Biddy just stood there solemnly and silently, waiting until they had finished. She would not talk about it, but scolded me when I dared to show my curiosity, saying that they were only poor little creatures and I ought to think how lucky I was and learn to mind my own business.

This was easy to do, because there was no playing about on the way home from school as there had been in Takapuna. Everyone went straight home, for all of the children had daily jobs to do about the farm and several had to help with the milking after a long ride on what was always the oldest, saddest horse on the farm. There were no school buses in the district and because of petrol rationing there was no possibility of being collected by the standard Waikato farmer's car: a Chevrolet or a Ford V8.

However, the prestige of riding to school was a compensation that every child was conscious of. There was a horse paddock next to the school and all classes ended half an hour earlier than town schools so that the pupils could catch and saddle up their half-blind broken-winded mokes. This distinction made the children feel a cut above mere 'townies' – which was the lowest class of being in the whole world. Even the damned in hell would look down on a townie.

There was another far more subtle peculiarity that gave country children a feeling of appalled superiority over townies, and that was in the matter of footwear. Country children wore proper boots all the time, summer and winter, whereas townies – at least in the Auckland of my childhood – made it a point of honour to go barefoot, even on the roughly metalled streets of Takapuna, and our feet were always covered in stone bruises to prove it.

Many is the time that my brother and sisters and I would leave by bus and ferry for 'town' (which pretty well meant Queen Street) properly dressed, but as soon as we got to the top of Rewhiti Avenue we would slip off our sandals or shoes and socks, and hide them in a hedge ready to put on again when we returned home. That the main street of the largest city in the Dominion was filled with urchins who chose to go barefoot was something that country children discussed with puzzled horror, and I was careful not to offend local practice by ever being seen in public with my feet uncovered.

Almost immediately after my arrival, I had the good luck to become close friends for a few months with a boy who lived close by on a neighbouring farm – until his father sold up and the family moved north, and the nearest child of my own age to play with then became a boy who lived a kilometre away.

This sudden change meant that for well over a year, apart from one school holiday when I was sent home, and the other school holidays when my brother and sister came to stay, I entered a strange land peopled by beings in games or adventures that existed solely in my imagination, or who stepped magically and fully alive out of the pages of the dozens of books I devoured voraciously – often in circular fashion, turning from the last page straight back to the first and reading the whole thing over and over again.

Each of these characters was real. In no sense were they coloured cardboard figments of my imagination. They were three-dimensional. They cast shadows and were made of flesh and blood. We played games together. They would put their arms over my shoulders, like any other friend, and confide in me. They instructed me in the use of passwords and summoned me by secret names. Their company gave me my first regular exercise in imaginative 'otherness'.

It would be absurd to claim that separation, isolation and loneliness in childhood are necessary determining factors in the making of a writer, but so many of those who have ended up as writers have described how some profound experience of solitariness or apartness when young has encouraged the development of a literary turn of mind, that it seems to be curiously influential. I know that the time I spent with Mac and Biddy was vitally important to me. It probably did nothing to help me socially or intellectually, but it threw down walls in the brain to let in a light which would radiate through all my days.

Just as important, the same removal process also allowed in grim shadows that could sometimes terrify me, but which I have never regretted. I still fumble in those occasional darknesses, and I am still reassured that I have not been able to locate their limits. They no longer frighten me, but they fill me with a prickly, shivering awareness of mystery and a mute, skulking sense of the unknowable.

23: KNOWLEDGE IN THE BLOOD

Throughout the whole of my childhood I think I met only the one boy whom I could describe as utterly beyond the help even of a teacher as brilliant and determined as Biddy. He was the boy on the neighbouring farm who was soon to be moving on, and I felt honoured to become his friend for the short time I knew him.

This anti-prodigy's name was Alan, and though it is easy now to recognise how secretly attractive his uncompromising resistance to my aunt's determined efforts must have seemed to me at the time, I didn't have the insight to be fully aware of this factor. He was willing to associate himself with me, despite the fact that I was a 'townie', and that was enough.

Alan's absolute refusal to learn wasn't a case of being dull, for he was quite the opposite; it was simply that he was astutely single-minded about his nature and the inevitability of his fate. He was only ten years old, yet he seemed to be more ancient than anyone I had ever known. In some strange way it seemed that he belonged to the land and the long ages of its transformations and the plants that have grown in its soil and the animals that have foraged over it or flown in the air above it.

School had no meaning to him. It was merely a place of occasional incarceration that he would one day be old enough to be allowed to escape from. There was nothing he could be taught by Biddy that he wanted to know. His family had 'sometime' come from 'somewhere' in England, where they had always been farmers – and farmers were all they would ever be.

As Alan explained his situation, in a phrase that mystified and thrilled me, farming was 'in his blood'. Immediately I could picture his heart pumping this strange rural liquid through his body. It was green and sludgy, and it smelled of cows and horses. I hoped he would cut himself sometime, though not too badly, and that I would be fortunate enough to be there to see what it really looked like.

His father, whom he always referred to a 'me old man', was illiterate, except to the extent that, when he had to, he could close one eye, clench his teeth, clutch a pen in his fist and slowly scratch out the few connected letters of his name. Alan's mother – 'me old woman' – could not even manage this feat, but I never got an answer to my questions about whether his uncommunicative but compulsively grinning elder brother could read and write. All enquiries about this mysterious member of the family were always deflected by the repeated assertion that he would be 'all right' so long as 'no one was silly enough to ask him to wipe the smile off his face'.

Alan's two sisters could both manage to decipher the statements and accounts that occasionally came in the mailbox, and that was about all, but it was enough of an accomplishment for Alan to maintain that it meant that only one of them could 'go out and get married' because the other would have 'to stay home with me and the rest of us and read the bloody bills and invoices'.

The family were good farmers, in an easygoing, plodding way. The old man was wonderful with animals and knew all sorts of country cures for them, and was a confident surgeon as well. He also knew the value of a picnic as an incentive for a mass attack on the Californian thistles that plagued the place. He would clean off his heavy sledge and hitch up his two glorious part-Clydesdales, one a half-draught and the other a very compact and intelligent quarter-draught that could open just about any gate on the farm, and I would join the whole family on a trip over the paddocks, where we'd boil the billy and scoff the bread and scones that Alan's mother would have prepared in the early morning, for she was a wonderful baker. Then we'd all fan out and pour small scoops of quicklime into the middle of each thistle.

Gorse, ragwort and blackberry joined the thistles in a savage war with the farmers for control of the land. There were no selective sprays in those days, so it was hand-to-hand combat, in a never-ending struggle.

But that wasn't the only work for a boy. It was Alan's daily duty to take the dogs and bring in the cows for milking, and he helped his father, mother and brother morning and night in the cowshed. Because I knew nothing of country life, it seemed unbelievable to me that a boy should have so much grown-up responsibility and I regarded it as a great privilege when, shortly after my arrival, Alan asked if I'd like to help him with the cows after school.

As it turned out, it was a lucky chance, for it opened the door to a whole existence that I would otherwise never have entered.

'What's your favourite tobacco?' Alan asked me as soon as we had dropped over the first ridge and were out of sight of the farm buildings.

I told him I didn't smoke.

Alan spat into the dirt then rubbed his boot in it. 'Do you know what means?' he demanded, and when I confessed that I didn't he said contemptuously, 'That's what I think of bloody townies.'

'Why?' I asked.

''Cos they don't bloody smoke,' he said, adding this new charge to the already insurmountable defects of not riding horses to school and not wearing proper boots.

I knew I'd failed some important test, and I desperately wanted him to stop thinking of me as a townie, so I described to him how my

UNDER THE BRIDGE & OVER THE MOON

grandfather smoked cigars and navy plug, which he had to cut with a pocket knife and rub in the palms of his hands before stuffing into his pipe, and how my aunt Biddy smoked Greys, Pocket Edition or Melrose roll-your-owns, depending on what was available.

'Does she smoke Riverbed Mould?' Alan asked, and when I said I'd never heard of that tobacco, he told me that was what all 'real smokers' like himself called Riverhead Gold, which was named after a famous racehorse and had a drawing of the horse next to the label, 'So you could say it's the only tobacco in New Zealand with a picture of the factory on the bloody packet, couldn't you?' he added.

This was a joke that I would later hear applied to Camel and several other brands of cigarettes and tobacco, but at the time I thought Alan must be the wittiest boy in all creation. My laughter seemed to appease him, for he yelled at the dogs to 'Get away back, you mongrel whoo-ers' and invited me to sit down beside him in the shelter of the ridge and he'd show me 'how to roll a fag so you can't tell the difference with a bloody tailor-made'.

When we were settled, he shifted a stone that covered a secret hole in a small bank nearby. He reached inside then pulled out a tin which contained tobacco, Zigzag cigarette papers and wax matches.

'I always sit here and bloody smoke. Every day, after bloody school,' he announced. 'And from now on you bloody can too.'

What about bringing in the cows? I asked him, and to my surprise he answered that it didn't really matter whether the bloody dogs bothered to go away back or not, for as soon as the cows spotted him or heard him yelling from the ridge they had to come in to be milked or their udders bloody crucified them with the weight of the bloody milk. 'So what else would I do, but sit here and bloody smoke?' he said.

And that was the end of the discussion. At the age of nine I became a regular smoker and under Alan's tutelage began to steal for the first time in my life, sneaking strands of tobacco from Biddy's packets and carefully fluffing up the remainder so my plunderings would never be missed — as they never were.

Alan also, more usefully, taught me how to saddle a horse or put the chains on them or back them into wagon-shafts, how to feed a calf, milk by hand, put the cups on a cow's teats, wash a separator, hose down the cowyard, feed pigs, yell at dogs and all the other routines that were simply part of his everyday world, but which were huge adventures for me. Alan used to shake his head and laugh at my bumbling efforts to learn his skills, for he could not remember ever having acquired them. They were simply things that were done by a boy brought up on a farm. They were part of the natural order of rural existence. It was as if he had never been subjected to learning processes, but had been born with a store of memories about the way things had to be gone about. It was a gift of knowing that belonged to all true country folk.

This secret country knowledge sometimes had strange applications, perhaps none more surprising than the day we were sent out to the hills at the back of the farm to inspect a fence that a bull had brought down. We walked some way down the road to take a shortcut, and as we turned a corner Alan stopped me suddenly by pulling at my jumper.

'Birds,' was all he said.

I looked ahead and saw a flock of sparrows fluffing up their feathers in the dust of the road. There was nothing remarkable in that.

'Do you want to see how to catch them in your bare hands?' he whispered.

I told him it was impossible. 'Birds can fly off,' I pointed out.

'Nah,' he said. 'Watch me.'

And with that he sprang forwards and ran full-pelt at the sparrows. Of course, they flew up and I was already prepared to laugh the whole thing off as a joke, but to my surprise he had frightened them straight at a clay bank where the road took a sharp turn. He raced straight up the almost sheer wall of clay and snatched into the air, then let himself slide down. In his hands he had a sparrow and a thrush.

'Bloody thrush,' he said proudly. 'I didn't see it till I put them up. I could've missed the bastard.'

It was the most amazing display of predatory skills I'd ever seen. It was as though he'd become in mind and body a wild animal himself. What, I asked him, was he going to do with the birds?

Alan looked at me in disbelief. How could I be so stupid? he seemed to be asking.

'This is what you do,' he said. And with that he slipped his fingers up and over the necks of the birds, and whirled them around in his hands, until he gave a final flick that flung their bodies onto the road. Then he opened his palms and showed me their two tiny heads.

'Easy, eh?' he said.

24: THE BAYSWATER FERRY-BOAT

When the school holidays came around I was sent home for a short break, though the thought of returning worried me for some reason I couldn't define. Children can sense when there's something nasty going on, even if adults don't bother to explain it to them.

For the moment I was happy to be with Biddy in her little one-roomed school at Cambridge, and with Mac and the great recitations and songs he would perform every night of the week after we'd eaten and done the dishes. Why should I want to leave the security and pleasure of crawling up on his huge barrel chest and feeling the quake of his words and tunes rippling right through me? And I was delighted with Alan, and the way he was teaching me the mysteries of country life and the satisfaction of sitting down in the shelter of a ridge and having a smoke while the dogs brought in the cows. Besides, I'd stopped pissing my bed. So why go home where something wonky was happening?

Sure enough, I got the whole works just after I got to Auckland. My mother and brother and sisters met me at the railway station and hardly anything was said as we caught the penny tram to Queen Street. It was only as we were all sitting on the Bayswater ferry that Mit finally dropped the bombshell.

'If Dad and Mum get a divorce, who are you going with?' he asked bluntly.

I couldn't speak, but looked at my mother. From her handbag she took out a little lace handkerchief. It was the same terrible article that she always carried with her when we went off to a meeting together. At some stage of the journey I could guarantee that she would spit on a corner of it before dabbing or rubbing at some spot of dirt I'd picked up on my face or hands. But this time she used it to wipe the corners of her own eyes.

She refused to look back at me. She was also unable to talk. This was the woman who could make great speeches and argue the toss with Jesuit priests. Suddenly she couldn't even pick up and throw back a remark from a seven-year-old boy.

Mit went on, 'I'm going with Dad. So's Ann. And Carole's going with Mum. Are you going with Mum, too?'

'Yes,' I managed to squeeze out of some part of my anguish and confusion.

'That's fair then,' Mit observed. 'One boy and one girl each. That's fifty-fifty.'

I nodded, but was still too choked to be able to talk.

Then my brother leant nearer and said in a mutter loud enough for all to hear, 'Except I don't really think it's a fair deal. 'Cos Dad's okay to live with, but you got the bitch.'

Poor little Mit, being the last born and arriving only thirteen months after Carole, had never had his rightful share of affection. He'd had to assert himself fearlessly to get a share of attention, and perhaps even earn a cuddle or two. He had to be ready to front up and insult and smash the lavatory pan off the floor to force the world to be bothered to acknowledge his existence – let alone to discover that he had a warm heart and a first-class brain in his head.

My mother had focused her declining love on myself and my sisters, and there was nothing but exhaustion and exasperation left for Mit. Most of her real energy went directly into the grand designs and objectives of the Rationalist Association and John A. Lee's Democratic Labour Party.

Mit's reaction to the habitual treatment he got from the very day he was born was to come out fighting. It now amazes me how someone at such a disadvantage in size, experience and verbal skills, could work out so cleverly that there was something unjust about the way the world was treating him – and decide that he was bloody well not going to put up with it. I had been totally blind, in my childhood selfishness, to the true order of things around me. I had been a glutton for all the love that was going and Mit had got only the leftovers. It was totally unfair, not least because he was a guileless undemanding loving little boy. In every sense of the word, Mit was deprived, and this deprivation took sometimes violent forms.

For instance, I adored my mother and would have done anything she asked, but if she told Mit to stand up or sit down and he didn't feel like doing so he would tell her to 'bugger off'. If she argued with him or hit him – and she could be formidable in both respects – he would work himself into a fury of swearing. His favourite expression for her was 'the great bitch'.

No child swore in front of their mothers like that in those days – and certainly not *at* them – and the punishment was terrible. My mother would trot out a catch-phrase that has now acquired a humorous overtone from being associated with a television comedy series: 'Wait till your father comes home.' But there was nothing funny about the threat when I was young. My father would get back from work and he would listen to the one-sided evidence in the matter of Mit's swearing, then he would deal out summary retribution.

My father would always trot out another favourite catch-phrase of the time, which I was later to hear many fathers repeat when womenfolk complained of their children's free employment of words that were supposed to be reserved for adult male use only. This article of faith and fair judgement went: 'If there's any swearing to be done in this house, I'll do it, okay?' And it was usually followed by a good beating.

Mit must have heard those words enough times to be able to repeat them backwards in his sleep. They were as silly as the brutal and utterly ineffective punishment that came as part of the grown-up package. Sometimes, after stubbornly repeated transgressions for the same offence, Mit qualified for the ultimate punishment, which was to have his mouth washed out with salt or sprinkled with pepper. The pain must have been searing, but it was as useless as all the other deterrents. The very next day, it would be back to all-out war again, with my mother yelling at him why did he have to be such a horrid little boy, followed by his inevitable instruction to her to 'bugger off, you bitch'.

So that was the way it was. I can picture it all now. We were side by side in the second row of the upper deck on the starboard side of the ferry. Ann was sitting there, full of wisdom and confidence. Carole, biting her lips. And Mit asking the questions.

My mother was wearing a fox-fur over her shoulders. Its hard glassy eyes were boring into me. They neither looked away nor blinked. They were dead. They just kept on staring and staring. And the evil grin of the fox seemed to have something to do with the way I was being asked to take sides.

The question that Mit had asked me was to torment me then and later. How could anyone expect even a grown-up person to be able to decide, just like that? So how then should a child be thought capable of an answer – a child who had only just been taught how to roll a cigarette by a boy who could run up a vertical wall of clay and pluck birds out of the air?

25: THE COLOUR PURPLE

I have crowded and precise memories of my life up till that moment on the Bayswater ferry when Mit asked me which side I would take if our parents divorced. After which, my memory is entirely selective. There are moments that I can recollect with what seems to be perfect clarity, but the packed succession of images suddenly ceases. There are great unexplained gaps, and I'm glad of them.

I think what happened was that, over the next ten or so years, I gradually entered into a stubbornly self-induced dream state, a protective imaginative cocoon constructed from earlier recollections and the books I read. It's a simple and entirely sensible defence mechanism.

There is not one memory that remains with me of what must have been the fortnight's school holiday break I spent at home – the last time we were ever to be together as a family. It has been erased entirely, though it can only have been charged with fear, and fraught with accusation and pleading. All I remember is being back in the little isolated Cambridge school once more, with Mac and Biddy, where I knew I was secure in their affection, in a place of books and daily routine, where the ground didn't seem as though at any moment it would crack open, and where everyone was safe from being sucked into the molten core of the Earth.

Then came the terrible news that Alan's father had sold their farm and a young childless couple were taking over. I hung about the cowshed moping about how I was losing the only friend I had to play with, but Alan was extremely cheerful and as he left he gave me a piece of brilliant misinformation that still makes me laugh.

'Do you want to know something before I go?' he asked importantly. Of course I did.

'What colour is the knob of your cock?'

I told him I thought it was a kind of pink-purple.

'Well, watch out it doesn't go all-purple then,' he said.

I asked him why not.

'Because when you go to the doctor's, he'll take one look at your knob and if it's purple he'll know straight away you've being doing it.'

'Doing what?' I wanted to know.

'Never mind,' he said. 'Just keep your bloody eye on your knob. That's all I'm telling you.'

I begged him to explain the mystery to me, but his only answer was to shake his head gravely and triumphantly.

'Well,' I said finally, 'what colour's your knob then?'

'Purple,' Alan said with a hysterical laugh. 'Deep, dark purple.'

I must have been a far too serious and gullible small boy, because I worried for months afterwards that I may be afflicted with a secret change of colour and accused by some outraged medical practitioner of something that I didn't know anything about. It was a wonderful practical joke, though when I eventually woke up to it I never had the heart to try it on some other poor little innocent.

The loss of Alan's company was made up for with a marvellous discovery when the new couple arrived. By this time I had read every book on the shelves of the farmhouses throughout the district – though the total couldn't have been that spectacular. Nearly every house had a Bible, a *Pears Cyclopedia*, an *Edmonds Cookery Book* or *Aunt Daisy's New Cookery*, and often not much besides. But every now and again a pile of cowboy books or other pulp fiction would turn up and I would devour them all with an indiscriminate ravenous appetite, so the first question I asked the new couple, while they were still unpacking, was whether by any chance they had a book or two I could borrow.

Books? It turned out they had cases and cases of them. The man had been a bookworm as a boy and had stored and looked after every precious volume he had ever owned. He hoped to have a son one day himself, he told me, and in the meantime he would lend me five at a time and when I returned each lot I could select another five.

I dug out James Fenimore Cooper's *The Last of the Mohicans* and *The Deerslayer*, plus a great assortment of books by Captain Frederick Marryat, Captain W.E. Johns, Rachel Compton, Sir Walter Scott, R.M. Ballantyne and all the wonder of an endless variety of 'Tenderfoot' books – he must have had fifty of them alone – to go with my all-time favourites, the endlessly pored-over *Huckleberry Finn* and *Robinson Crusoe*.

My life was suddenly peopled with a whole new gang of friends. I was surrounded with pilots, sailors, pirates, knights in armour, Red Indians, cowboys and resourceful desperadoes of all kinds. I wandered over prairies, huge forests and desert islands, through great walled cities of old, up and down the Mississippi River and across the airways and oceans of the world. That little isolated Waikato valley, with its paddocks, creeks and bush-clad hills, where only the timid deer would invade the clearings at dawn, became a place of brilliant, riotous, dangerous tumult. My life was unbounded.

26: THE CHINA CABINET

Although Mac refused to attend the monthly non-denominational church service in the school, and stated that he was only too willing to make his views on the notion of a deity perfectly plain if any bugger thought fit to question him, Biddy always dressed up in her best suit, hat and gloves, and went along. She confided in me that her attendance was expected of her as the sole teacher of the community's children, and in any case it was the polite thing to do, even if she had to admit in strict confidence that the itinerant preachers who ranted in her school were poor trash and charlatans.

Biddy was respectability personified. Even though she was a small and trim person, she used to force herself into corsets, so that she couldn't help strutting about like a mechanical doll. These weird instruments of self-torture would sway stiffly and ponderously on the clothesline, every washing day, out of sight from passers-by, at the back of the schoolhouse. They were grotesque garments, coloured pale peach or orange, reinforced with what seemed to be metal struts, and with long laces threaded criss-cross through a series of eyelets. I found them fascinating and hilarious, and tried to picture how she fitted into them. A bit like lacing herself into an old boot, I thought.

She was not only fastidious in her appearance, but followed the strange custom of the time (which my mother and father had long before abandoned) of turning the sitting room, or 'front room' as it was usually called in the country, into a sanctum sanctorum. Under Biddy's regime, our front room became a forbidden territory to the males of the household, even on rare occasions of social ceremony when visitors were allowed in.

Within the dim though glossy polished depths of this holy place were several objects that I sometimes sneaked in to gaze at. Hanging on chains from the walls were a couple of heavy mirrors, a floral tapestry that

Biddy had made and a large and ornately framed print of Franz Hals's 'Laughing Cavalier'. There was also a corner bookcase, which actually held a selection of fragile pieces of china and glassware between a few dozen expensively bound editions of the poems of Byron, Shelley, Keats, Hood, Cowper and Longfellow, the complete works of Shakespeare, a large Bible, and works by eighteenth and nineteenth-century writers, from Defoe to Dickens. These books, I was astonished to discover, were not meant to be read; their pages were flimsy and their fonts were tiny. It was the gold-lettered bindings and the prestige of their authors' names that were meant to be looked at and admired.

But the main feature of the room was a glass-fronted item of furniture referred to as 'the china-cabinet', in which were displayed certain holy relics of cut glass and painted porcelain that, like the books, were never meant to be used. At the corners of the 'Persian' carpet that occupied the precise centre of the room, were four very uncomfortable chairs, sporting expensive upholstery which was protected by antimacassars.

When I rode over to visit other farms, I discovered that this was the country rule. There was always a room kept aside, spotlessly dusted and polished, and glittering with collections of decanters, bowls and glasses, always referred to collectively as 'crystal', and gorgeous teapots and dainty cups and saucers that were hardly ever used. The room was a representation of the ideal, a place of perfection that contrasted with the mud and stench of the farm, a sanctuary devoted to household gods where the womenfolk kept out the men.

I saw Biddy's front room used only twice, once for some reason after church and once when the school inspectors paid a visit. Otherwise the social centre of the house was the kitchen, with its double focus – the range that Mac would light every morning sharp at six, and where I would station myself soon afterwards to stir the breakfast porridge; and the radio, whose valves would bring us the 'war news', parliamentary debates and the joy of keeping up with 'the serials' – nightly episodes in the lives of the everlasting suburban nitwits *Fred and Maggie*, the folksy *Dad and Dave of Snake Gulch*, and even the terrifying evildoers who made such epics as *Bulldog Drummond* such a delight – all of which had been forbidden in Takapuna.

Altogether, our life in the country had an order that was quite different from the city existence I was used to. The three people who lived in the schoolhouse, Mac, Biddy and myself, belonged to three different generations, so we communicated in linear fashion through time, without sharing lateral experiences.

Mac lived in the dream world of his lost farming empire in Whangamomona, which had been the crowning achievement of the great adventure of his life and had now become part of a more general sense of Irish disappointment, grievance and resentment – and all of it completely and cussedly at odds with his vision of a worldwide Communist takeover where there would never again be individual owners of land.

Biddy inhabited a world of work and ambition, held together by personal propriety, embroidery, a china cabinet and masterworks of the art of corsetry. And I became an only child in a universe of books and adult adulation and exhortation.

The only thing wrong with the whole perfect arrangement was that I was still a runt and refused to grow, even though I was forced to traipse over to the neighbouring cowshed every night to drink a jug of frothy full-cream milk, straight from the udder, in order to encourage my body to shape up.

Yet inwardly I thrived. Mac and Biddy were like parents to me, and in their stern proud puritan way they loved me and made me the centre of their attention. Though I didn't know it at the time, they did not want to give me back. They knew, much better than I did, what was going on in Takapuna, and they had made plans to keep me.

It is now amusing to think of it this way, but the truth of the arrangement they had worked out between themselves was that I had ascended through the ranks of family to become the substitute son of my aunt and grandfather. It was very tribal and very Irish.

Biddy and Mac had become jealous in their guardianship, and they probably thought, in their adult fashion, that I was unaware of this. The other children in the family were acceptable to them as visitors, but it became quite clear to me (and to my brother and sisters) that they were not in the same category of immediate dependency that I had been adopted into. Carole and Mit came down a couple of times to stay in the school holidays, and the absurdity of our contrasting situations was as apparent to us then, as it was to be in later years.

Whereas I would never be anything other than a spectator of country matters, Carole was good at cooking, sewing and all the rural arts expected of a girl; and as for Mit, well, he was a natural. Immediately he arrived he got on the back of a horse and almost had to be prised off in the evenings. He was a country boy through and through – and life came full circle for him about twenty years ago when he and his wife Jocelyn bought a farm, in Tahekeroa, where they still run cattle today.

There was one unforgettable, almost miraculous, incident that took place not long after Mit came down, which seems to me to throw clear light on the contradictoriness of the set-up. Like Mac, and Mac's father before him, Mit was fearless with horses, and the faster they went the better he liked them. To show Mac how well he could ride, he asked him to come to the front fence of the schoolhouse and watch as he galloped by on an old racehorse that he'd borrowed from a neighbouring farmer. I liked riding and I loved horses, but it was not something I would ever have bothered (let alone dared) to do.

I stood there beside Mac and watched my young brother hurtle down the road, crouched on the saddle, his head nestling into the mane, his knees high on shortened stirrup-leathers, just like a young jockey. He didn't have to be taught how to do it; he was born with the knack.

But the horse still had a test to make before it was going to let a child command it, and just before they passed by, when Mit reined in, the horse answered the bit as if it had been trained to halt stock-still on a sixpence. Of course, when the horse stopped, Mit just kept on going. He flew through the air in a perfect arc, performing a full double somersault on the way. It was like a circus performance – hair-raising, perilous, spectacular.

It was only afterwards that I realised that Mit could have hurt himself badly or even broken his neck; but what happened next took all my attention. It took only a few seconds but was one of the most extraordinary and graceful physical acts I have ever witnessed. Mac made a swift sideways movement to place himself in position, then held out both arms, and with all the style and accuracy of an All Black fullback caught his grandson from the sky. He clutched the boy against his chest then lowered him gently to the ground, where Mit didn't know whether to burble his surprise at the treachery of the horse that had thrown him or at the way his grandfather had so wondrously saved him.

Mac dusted the boy off and said to him severely, 'Get straight back on that nag, you silly young bugger, or he'll always know he's got you beat. Go on, get back in the saddle and show him who's boss.'

Mit did and the horse never pulled that trick on him again.

27: WHISPERS

One night I woke in a panic to hear voices through my bedroom wall. The sound was subdued, but urgent. All I could pick out from the buzz of conversation were repeated phrases which went something like: 'She didn't! . . . He didn't! . . . What did *he* say? . . . What did *she* say?'

Moya and Sheila had made a lightning visit, and since it was a time when travel was made difficult by stringent petrol rationing, that had to mean something very important was up, something so frightening that it couldn't be discussed in front of me over the evening meal.

I put an ear to the wallpaper, just below where I had proudly pinned the giant Jesus card and the smaller four-evangelists cards I had earned by never failing to attend the Sunday School classes which were held either outside in the playground or in the saddle shed while the once-a-month church services took place inside the school building.

These cards had been given to me by the young, plump, mad-eyed woman of about fifteen or sixteen who ran the classes and was the main attraction of them. She claimed to know every word written in the Bible, but none of the handful of children paid much attention to the boast. Her most impressive accomplishment so far as we were concerned was an involuntary one: she would suddenly and with no warning stare wildly at one of us and her face would be immediately suffused with scarlet blushes. She also intrigued us by wearing print frocks, with long sleeves and buttons up to the neck, which were too small for her, and which were just about bursting at the seams from the pressure of the ever-increasing and embarrassing bulges of her body that for some mysterious reason she seemed to be trying to deny.

But I wasn't thinking of this interesting young woman as I listened to the voices murmuring through the wall. I knew something terrible was being discussed and that it had to do with my father and mother.

There was no electric light to switch on in the room I was in, and the candle had been snuffed, but a glow of moonlight came through the window. I looked up from the pillow and there above me I saw the cards the young woman had given me.

It was like a miracle. There was Jesus. I didn't think of an appropriate form of address, but just blurted out to Him directly what was on my mind: 'I swear I'll be a good boy, Jesus, and I'll stop pinching Biddy's tobacco, if only You'll tell me what's going on.'

There was no reply, so I peed the bed in panic.

It was the first time I had done so since coming to live with Mac and Biddy, but it was certainly not the last. I was soon to give up even trying to control myself, in a last explosive and spectacular exhibition of weakness. The Shame of Takapuna, the Freak with the Woolworth's Bladder was about to stage his final great performances.

In guilt and confusion I tried again to summon help from Jesus. But in the moonlight His eyes just gazed down on me blankly from the wall, refusing to light up and comfort me as the young woman with the bulges had promised. Indeed, now that I came to search His expression more closely, I was struck by something I had not noticed previously. Jesus looked bored and almost stunned. He had a kind of bleary unfocused half-smile, as if He had just been clocked over the head or had been drinking out of a bottle wrapped in a paper bag, like the 'methos' in Albert Park. So when I thought about it, it hardly surprised me that He had disdained to answer my appeal.

There was something apathetic about His appearance which I had no way of interpreting, though years later the long hair, curly sideboards and the caftan would explain everything. As I kept on staring at Him, with the stench of urine rising from the blankets, it seemed to me that if He was ever going to be bothered to send me a message, it would only be to drawl out of the side of his mouth: 'Don't waste my time sonny boy – okay?'

Then through the wall I heard the fatal words: 'She's left him,' followed after a few minutes by the distinct words, pronounced in a hoarse whisper, 'This time it's for good. There's no going back . . .' I couldn't make out more than that, but after a while I heard Moya stammer out loud that, 'There could have been a m-m-murder, if-if-if they'd g-g-gone on like that . . .'

Then Biddy and Sheila both said, 'Keep your voice down. You'll wake the boy,' and Sheila added, 'It's always the same. Have we ever lived in a house where the walls didn't have big ears?'

How near the literal truth she was. My ear was now shoved so hard against the wall that the whole house began to echo like the roar of the waves in a seashell. I gave up and slumped miserably asleep.

The next morning there was hell to pay when I reported the wet sheets. Biddy threatened me with the dreaded rubber undersheet that

I'd been sent with and which I'd forgotten about. It was the disgusting item that my father had made me lie on when I had practised my first efforts in emotional regression into babyhood at Takapuna.

As it turned out, Biddy's initial reluctance to force me to use the sheet and her hope that she would persuade me by reason alone to come to my senses 'and behave like a normal respectable boy' had a memorable effect on my mattress. It used to be dragged outside in the sun to be aired, and it acquired a series of stains that revealed varying high-tide marks, which depended on either the fullness of my bladder or whether I was able to wake up when I began peeing and make a dash outside. These marks interestingly came to resemble the annual growth-rings to be found on a cross-section of the trunk of a tree. I became fascinated by all aspects of the helpless hypnotic compulsion I suffered from, though in no way did this balance out the embarrassment I suffered.

But on the morning after Moya and Sheila's sudden arrival my demonstration of how to turn a mattress into a botanical wonder had only a shortlived notoriety compared with the real news that was delivered to me in short bursts over breakfast. Since there was no telephone in the schoolhouse, Moya and Sheila had come all the way from Auckland to tell Biddy that my mother had left Takapuna to stay with a woman friend in Papatoetoe, she had taken Carole with her and she would be coming to collect me just as soon as she had a job and some proper accommodation.

These items were gradually presented to me by my aunts, mixed in with repeated accusations about what ungrateful little devils Ann and Mit were to have chosen to stay with their father, and with elaborate reassurances that Carole and I were the lucky ones because once everything was worked out we could nestle under the wing of our mother again.

I looked at Biddy and she looked back directly and intently at me. Her expression was one I have never forgotten. It was one of those moments when you become aware that you are being deceived by those you trusted. I could see it in her look. She wasn't telling the truth. She wasn't ever going to give me up, to my mother or father – or anyone else in the longer term either.

It was only after she had rolled a cigarette, and complained in passing that she'd have to give up smoking if she continued to rip through tobacco at that rate, that she announced very sensibly and firmly that it was her opinion that it would be a long time before Claire was in a

UNDER THE BRIDGE & OVER THE MOON

position to look after two children, and in the meantime one would be quite a handful, so things could continue as they were at present, well into the foreseeable future so far as she was concerned.

Moya and Sheila nodded their heads. They were not going to upset a perfectly good arrangement. They were in full agreement with Biddy. I should continue to live with her and their father, and in a year or so Biddy would have finished her country service. Then, with her inevitably superb grading marks, she would be able to take a top job with no salary bar and she could well afford to send me to the best secondary school in the land, and after that to university, where I would honour her sacrifices by becoming an illustrious academic success.

In the meantime I decided to crawl back into my shell and go on pissing myself and wondering how the world came to be in such a terrible state. It seemed that the natural order of things was that the children were born to be divided up by the grown-ups, who never felt obliged to tell the truth or explain anything or even to see that the children's viewpoints might just possibly be taken into account.

But, of course, I was personalising the situation. Matters were far more dramatic and tormented for my brother and sisters than the mere uncertainty through which I lived, with the sinister claims that were being made on my allegiance. I was later to find out that by living in the country I had been spared the terror of the night of the final split.

What happened, Ann told me later, was that my mother and father had an almighty row. There was screaming and yelling and accusations. Then my mother stopped altogether and calmly filled the electric jug and boiled it. My father thought she must be about to make a pot of tea, but instead she went up to him and tried to fling the jug into his face to blind him. Ann realised what was about to happen and leapt in front of my father. Both were badly scalded across their faces, arms and chests, but my father's eyes escaped injury. Without stopping to think he flipped my mother over his knee and gave her a hiding.

That evening marked the violent end of their marriage. There was soon to be a judicial separation, with an eventual decree nisi and absolute, but these were legal afterthoughts. The fact was that it all finished in a flash of searing water and a heavy hand.

Moya was right. Things couldn't have been much worse. And there really could have been a murder.

28: THE DREAM BULL

The Japanese were slowly being turned back across the Pacific, New Zealand soldiers had landed in Italy and the Russians were advancing towards Europe. The world outside looked a better and safer place.

The year was ending, my second summer in the country was on the way and the hay paddocks were almost ready for the day when the farming families, with their teams of half-draughts and rusty rattling machinery, would move around the valley from farm to farm mowing the long grass, raking and drying it, gathering it into sheaves, then into stooks, which would be heaved up on pitchforks by the strongest men, or raised by booms and pulleys, to build the giant haystacks that were once a feature of our countryside.

It would again be a time of picnics, neighbourliness, friendly rivalry, jokes and hard work, when no one ever asked the time and everyone kept an eye on the weather and bent their backs to beat the rain.

A couple of decades later, when the old handmade haystacks had gone, to be replaced by bales parcelled and bound by tractor-drawn machines, I was watching haymakers working up by Wellsford and I suddenly remembered a scene out of my childhood, as though in a photograph.

In that remembered Cambridge scene there was a cloud precisely like the one I was now looking at in Wellsford. Birds were perched on the fences and powerlines waiting to feast off the insects as the hay was swept up into the baler, just as they had been in my boyhood memory. A cat was there beneath a stand of pines, setting off to hunt the birds, in the way that farm cats always used to hang around at haymaking. And to clinch the scene, a hare leapt across the paddock, just as you'd sometimes see them working the grass stubble down in the Waikato. I superimposed these recollections of bustle and animal excitement on the scene before me and borrowed a title from a line in Christopher Marlowe's *Edward II*. The resulting poem is called 'Antic Hay':

> A lip-like cloud,
> pierced by the last shaft of the harvest sun,
> smiles inanely on the bristling fields
> and the newly parcelled hay.

An abacus of sparrows is numbered
on the strands of fences; starlings, like quavers,
dot the powerlines; and a counting cat
pricks through the needles of the pines.

And hills in the warm wind
dissolve in a storm of grass-sticks
and a hare weaves cockily
through the semi-solid air.

There are more personal memories of that summer – and with human actors, too. One that has never left me is of Mac out on a far hillside of the nextdoor farm, slashing ti-tree. It was the kind of unpaid, useful job he liked doing. He was proud of the way that even in his sixties he could almost effortlessly bowl over regenerating scrub by the acre, and I could see from the far distance, as I made my way towards him, the swathes of grey-brown sticks and foliage he had left in his wake.

Over my shoulder swung a bag which contained Mac's precious thermos flask full of hot tea, and a thick cheese-and-lettuce sandwich, plus a monster wedge of cake, for his lunch.

I followed a cattle track along a ridge then took a shortcut down into a scrubby gully – and my heart nearly stopped. As I pushed through the ti-tree I almost bumped straight into the Jersey bull that had a reputation for being the most crazy dangerous animal in the district. I stared right into its eyes. And they were mad all right.

I didn't even think about running. My legs made my mind up for me, and I found myself leaping a creek, stumbling over old stumps, dodging through more scrub – until at last I managed to scramble over a barbed-wire fence. I'd made it. It was safe to lie down and get my breath back. But then I discovered that the bull hadn't followed me. It wasn't there on the other side of the fence as it should have been. It had ignored me. The hoofbeats I'd heard behind me must have been the drumming of blood in my ears. Slowly I got up and took the long way around the ridge to deliver Mac's lunch. At least, I consoled myself, I'd done the right thing. You never took a chance with a Jersey bull. But it made me feel a bit silly just the same. I'd been running away from a phantom.

I said nothing about the incident to Mac as I handed him the bag, and we sat down together while he poured out the tea.

'Jesus Christ,' he shouted suddenly. 'What have you done to the thermos, you young brigand?'

I looked at the Bakelite beaker he held in one of his enormous paws. It was full of long splinters of broken glass. In my panic to escape the bull I must have stumbled and busted the bloody thing.

Mac was furious, and I told him how sorry I was – which was a genuine response – but I couldn't bring myself to explain what had really happened, for I simply had to get away for a while on my own to think about it. The shattered glass in the beaker seemed suddenly important. It reminded me of something I couldn't quite place and identify – almost as if represented a broken covering or membrane inside me.

Then I had it. Now that the glass was smashed to bits I could see inside myself, into a recurrent nightmare which I had suppressed for years, although I knew it had kept returning, often night after night (and would continue to do so until I was almost twenty).

The dream was a simple one; it is commonly reported in mythology, and Mary Renault used it in one of her recreations of life in ancient Greece. My version of it nearly always followed the same pattern. I would be either on a beach or in a paddock, and I would hear a loud roaring, as if a breaking wave or a high wind was sweeping towards me. I would turn and see a huge bull bearing down on me, head lowered, eyes bulging, nostrils steaming. Always there would be no chance of escape. Then just before 'the bull trampled and destroyed me I would wake up. The Greeks considered such dreams to be a manifestation of the gods, especially of Poseidon, though many psychiatrists nowadays would probably interpret them as projections of a father image. – and with hindsight I can see that my attitude towards my father was far more complex than I understood at the time and for decades to follow.

For years I had managed not to remember the nightmare in my waking hours: I had buried it and refused to deal with it. But the day's frightening meeting with the bull and the breaking of Mac's thermos had brought the haunting terror of the night to the surface. It was there and real, and I could no longer deny it.

Then two strange things happened. The first was something I didn't notice for some days, but it seemed like a great achievement in retrospect. I stopped wetting the bed. Just like that. The dream no longer had its old power over me.

And the second was that my father appeared as if by magic. He was sitting in the schoolhouse kitchen talking to Biddy and she had been crying.

29: A MAN AT A GATE

This was the first of three visits that my father made to Cambridge in quick succession. A few weeks previously he had brought Carole to stay temporarily with Biddy, Mac and myself. Mit had also arrived to join us. And now he appeared for a second time to collect all three of us and take us back to join Ann and himself at Takapuna.

Until this moment, Biddy had appeared to be running the school-house as a family refuge centre, but there was method in her charity. Carole's clothes had been forwarded secretly by my mother, so she was no temporary guest, whereas Mit's situation was never referred to even obliquely and he seemed to be merely being minded in transit to some vague and never-to-be-revealed destination.

The sisters' main plan had been simply for Biddy to keep as many of us as possible away from Takapuna, even though my mother had no way of looking after us herself for some time to come.

Obviously, Biddy and my father had been arguing, but when I walked into the room they stopped. Indeed, everything soon became amicable.

It is only with hindsight that it is possible to understand Biddy's determination and her cleverness at improvisation. She brightened up and became chatty, and in no time at all she began to agree with my father's wishes, and it was decided that Carole and Mit would return to Takapuna straight away, though I would stay on till Christmas with Biddy and Mac, so that my school year would not be messed up. Of course, this was nonsense, for I was only ten and no harm could possibly have been done, but it sounded plausible to my father who had left school at fourteen and felt he ought to defer to Biddy's expertise.

Biddy claimed to be entirely neutral in her attitude to the forthcoming divorce, and she must have put up a very convincing performance. After all, here she was – perfectly willing to hand over two of the three children in her care without further argument and with no more tears.

As for me, I recall only that I was content to go along with Biddy's new arrangement. After all, it flattered me and made me feel important.

However, a few weeks went by and my father suddenly turned up again. This time he had Ann with him and Biddy was taken by surprise, for she had thought he had used up all his petrol coupons and that she had plenty of time to make certain he would not be able to get near me again. But my father had been alerted by well-placed Catholic friends that, immediately after he had left with Carole and Mit, Biddy had made an approach to the Church in Hamilton to have me spirited away into the care of an orphanage, where I could be kept securely until it was safe for me to be returned to her. My father's friend Roy Agnew, who ran a taxi business, had slipped him a few gallons of petrol and he had jumped in the car and come immediately.

There was a hell of a row; but there was as much farce as tragedy. By chance, Biddy had looked out from the schoolhouse kitchen and seen my father's car coming. Quickly, and without telling me what was going on, she packed me off across the paddocks to a neighbouring farm. According to Ann, she then let loose all the words she had picked up from every little urchin in the playgrounds she had supervised, and like my mother, she too began to throw water at father and daughter – though fortunately it was cold.

Eventually I was found and fetched back, where I was stunned at the change in my father. The strain had now got to him and his face was lined and exhausted. But what astonished me most was that his skin had turned yellow. The man was clearly very ill. He should have been in hospital.

Biddy showed no sympathy. She was in a screaming fury and told me that my father, having already kidnapped Carole from Papatoetoe, was now trying to kidnap me; and that I was to tell him I didn't want to go, and that I wanted to stay in Cambridge with her and with Mac, where I was happy.

I must say my father handled the situation well. He said there was no question of a kidnap, for I was going to be the one to decide where I was going to live. Not Biddy. Not Mac. Not my mother. And not him. Just me.

He let the novelty of that statement sink in, then he asked me, 'Do you want to stay here and become Biddy's little boy, or do you want to come back and live with your family?'

Biddy didn't have the sense to shut up. She kept on trying to confuse matters and to call on Mac to grab hold of me and not let me be stolen from her.

Naturally, I said I wanted to go home.

'Don't be stupid,' she bawled in her most formidable schoolroom manner. 'I can't let you make such a big mistake. Don't you see how I'm turning you into somebody? You'll only waste your opportunities with those other dumb children. They'll drag you down.'

As arguments go she couldn't have trotted out a worse one. I loved my brother and sisters, and though I liked and responded to being the focus of Biddy's lavish attention, when she put the matter in the context of competitive claims, all she did was make her own position look twisted and threatening. There was now no way I was willing to stay. In fact, all of a sudden I knew I was going to get away from her as fast as I could go.

'I want to go home,' I remember shouting at her.

Biddy went on pleading and arguing. She said she was my guardian and my father would end in jail for what he was doing, and my mother had given orders for me to stay, and no one would ever be forgiven if I was allowed to be taken away like this. And she repeated over and over that legally my mother had a right to be heard, and that it would be better to hang on and see what she and the law courts decided was in my own best interests.

The more she went on, the more I was determined to get out of her clutches. I knew I'd go back to pissing my bed forever and I'd always be polite and pleased when other people decided what was best for me. Here was a chance to make up my own mind and do something decisive on my own account, and I certainly wasn't going to waste it.

'I want to go home,' I repeated. 'And that's final.'

At which point my father got up and said she'd heard what I'd said, so all we had to do was pack a few clothes and books, and then we'd be off.

We gathered up some things while Biddy hovered about, snatching pathetic bits of clothing out of my father's hands, saying he had no right to the good clothes she'd bought for me with her own money. And all the time she kept threatening that she was going to call the police as soon as she could get to a neighbouring farm where there was a telephone so she could report him for obtaining black market petrol, and she babbled on about lawyers and law courts and yelled at Mac, 'Bernard's trying to kidnap the boy. Help me stop him.'

The rest of my memory is confused, but I recall that at one stage Mac turned to me and said, 'So, Billy boy,' – for that was his endearment for me – 'what's your opinion in the matter? What do you really and truly want to do?'

I can remember looking at him and realising that I loved him and owed him more than anyone else in the world. But when that was weighed up against the place I still thought of. as 'home', with my brother and sisters in it, it simply wasn't enough to tip the balance.

With a hollow sense that I was betraying him, and with tears in my eyes, I said, 'I don't want to stay here any more.'

'And you don't feel that anyone is forcing you to do anything you don't want to do?'

'No,' I said.

'Well, I won't stand in your way then,' he said simply, and the tears were running down his cheeks too.

We took my little suitcase and a few books, and my father and I went out to the car and climbed in. Biddy wouldn't come out. She was still shouting and screaming from inside the house. But Mac followed us from the front door.

My last look at the little paradise they had tried so hard to make for me was of the man I adored standing there at the gate. My grandfather didn't move. He didn't wave, but just stared after us as we drove away.

Mac was wearing a pink woollen singlet and he had put on his bowler hat to make his farewell. But there had been no last words. After all the lunatic things that had been said that day, there was nothing that anyone could add without choking.

30: BLOOD EVERYWHERE

As the tiny Austin Seven rattled over the potholed metalled roads, my father harangued me with his version of events at home. In between each long and shocking episode of the break-up he would fire loaded questions at me, asking for exact details of how I had 'suffered' at the cruel hands of Biddy, how she had 'indoctrinated' me by 'forcing' me to go to Sunday school and how she had 'warped' my mind and turned me against him by coaching me in my mother's account of his impossible demands and behaviour.

The questions were nonsense, but a child has no chance against hours of such pressure and he constantly trapped me into comments and admissions that I hadn't meant to make. He would look at me, instead of at the road, and the tiny car would bounce and veer on its narrow spoked wheels from one side to the other, then every now and again he would swerve up to a farm gateway or onto a grass verge and produce a pad on which he would write down the false or lopsided evidence he had twisted out of me. I couldn't stand up to this relentless interrogation, so just went along with it.

His face was now sweating steadily and in the afternoon sunshine it began to glow with the yellow poisons that seemed to be working through his skin. I had never before seen a person in such a state of violent agitation. Clearly the strain he was under was making him not just physically ill; he was going – in the jargon of the time – right off his bloody rocker.

My father didn't cease talking for the whole long journey to Auckland. It was so alarming that I don't remember Ann being in the car at all, though perhaps this may have been because the strain had begun to affect her too. By the end of the journey she was quite ill, and she remained so for weeks afterwards.

The frequent stops to collect evidence and the compulsory wait at the top of the Bombay hills while the radiator boiled over then cooled down meant that the trip took an age, so it was well into the afternoon when suddenly my father pulled a master stroke. Instead of driving through Auckland to catch the vehicular ferry, we turned off westwards into the Waitakere ranges and headed for Cornwallis, where my Uncle Harold and his family always took their summer holidays.

The scene as we arrived at the campsite was unnerving. My cousins and my brother and younger sister were lolling about in the sun with blood dribbling from their mouths and splashing over their chests and bathing suits. There was blood everywhere. It was a scene of carnage and horror.

Except that they were shouting and laughing. I discovered that they were hoeing into a huge pot of boiled beetroot, peeling them and scoffing them like apples, with great hunks of white bread heaped with mighty slabs of butter. Beetroot juice was pouring all over them.

White bread! Slabs of butter! We probably scoffed a whole week's butter ration in that one sitting. Uncle Harold's holiday was over and he was working at his Balmoral shop: he would never have allowed us to eat rubbish like that. To us kids, white bread and butter was a treat, like cake. I tucked in straight away and the trip north from the country was made worthwhile. My father had begun to smile and joke again, I was back among my siblings, and I suddenly knew I was happy.

Here, at Cornwallis, I was under no pressure to play a role in a grown-up drama I couldn't comprehend. I was in a safe haven where no one gave a stuff if the beetroot juice ran all over them, provided they were enjoying themselves and the adults weren't arguing.

Today Cornwallis is a park, but it could easily have become yet another seaside suburb of Auckland. The baches that were beginning to creep along the main beach would have destroyed the coastline, but in the late 1930s and throughout the 1940s, the changes were slow and almost imperceptible. It was an idyllic time for those lucky enough to have a bach there, or a section on which to pitch a tent.

Harold had a section just behind the wharf; he later acquired a beautiful bach on the small headland that divided Cornwallis into two separate beaches at high tide. The wharf was a great place to fish for piper and sprats, and you could gaze down into the clear water and watch huge kingfish come in and nuzzle the piles. Around the point was a secret place we called the maomao rock, where we caught feasts of blue maomao, surely the most delicate-tasting fish in the sea. The sandbanks in the middle of the Manakau harbour were a dangerous source of scallops at very low tides, and children were taken out there only when there were plenty of adults around to keep an eye on them. It was a summer paradise.

Gaff-rigged scows with patched canvas sails still plied the coasts in those days. The crews used to shout to us across the water when we were out in the dinghy, then yell with laughter. I could never make out what they said, but my cousins convinced me that they were pirates and cutthroats who specialised in stealing small boys.

It was easy to believe this, for the men who worked the scows had tattoos and they wore ripped shirts, trousers held up by belts with fat buckles or lengths of rope, and they always sported peaked caps or white-spotted scarlet headscarves tied in a knot at the back. They were free spirits and I often wished they would come, as threatened, and carry me away to become one of their gang and save me from having to go to bed at the proper time every night while my cousins were out in the dinghy at sunset with some of the girls from nearby tents, drifting about, their hands dangling in the water, singing or yodelling and having the time of their lives.

Cornwallis was wonderful. It was a place of perfect happiness. The only cloud was Ann's illness. The holiday was spoiled for her, and my father drove her back to Epsom to stay with Harold, who nursed her back to health.

But soon enough we would be back together again as a makeshift family. The children had not been divided and shared out, and we were about to return to the security of our 'proper home' in Takapuna, where the garden was growing, the chooks were laying, and where the beach was just down at the bottom of the road and there were bags of fish to catch from the sea. Everything would be back to normal.

Well, sort of. We had lost our mother. She had taken off to find her own destiny and I would not see her again for almost a decade. She did one day pay Ann a visit at work – as upsetting as it was surprising – but that was an isolated event. And Carole and Mit have never seen her since the day they parted.

31: A VIEW FROM A PAPER-ROUND

As I have previously described, I managed to store away few connected memories from the events of the next years. I must have suffered a bout of selective amnesia. There are flashes of recollection, but they lack relevance. It is almost as if, for a while, I became an occasional observer of my life rather than an active participant; I supppose my brain jettisoned as junk a great deal of what was happening.

I think also that the dream state – the secretive other-world of books and fantasies that I largely chose to live in while I suffered my last couple of years at primary school, endured five years of secondary education and advanced into prolonged adolescence – came complete with its own set of unreliable incidents and interpretations, and its own values, based not on the militant and intolerant public morality that all children and young people were instructed in at the time, but on a contrived and private code shaped by a family background of political non-conformity and a personal sense of abandonment fed by my innate and furious stubbornness, and further complicated by the intense friendships I formed with any other boy who seemed to show signs, in some way, of being an 'outsider'.

With the advantage of age and experience, I now distrust such alternative codes. They are too inclined towards wild misapprehension, whimsical choice and erratic and unaccountable consequence. But at the time the way I viewed the world seemed to be founded on a fair apprehension of the patterns of what was taken for granted as normal suburban behaviour.

Strangely enough the memories that revealed such patterns remain perfectly clear to this day. But what makes my perception of those memories now seem downright puzzling is that most people I talk to seem to have disremembered them.

In other words, the situation is entirely reversed: I can remember very little of the day-to-day detail of my life, but I remember our public set-up – the moods and attitudes – with no trouble at all; whereas nearly everyone I speak to can recollect the yawn-inducing trivia of their dull years of schoolroom indoctrination, yet they not only don't remember what life in general was like, some are prepared vehemently to defend their monstrous illusions and deny the simple truth.

Ten years ago I wrote an essay for a book called *One of the Boys*, edited by Michael King, and it involved me in some controversy. I was bailed up in the street and accused of trying to spoil the happiness of people's memories, 'just because you think you had a bad time', and even my very tolerant sisters – among a great many others – told me I'd got the emphasis wrong. Yet I had done nothing more than invite people to look at the way we really were, not through the rose tints of nostalgia, but in plain fact.

The main point I made in the essay was that I grew up in a country which was conditioned by a code of deliberate, systematic and bloody-minded violence, and that this violence was visited with depraved enthusiasm on the children. The thing I neglected to say was that those who didn't bash each other or their kids were just as responsible for not doing anything about the violence as those who practised it.

Civilised and gentle people preferred not to notice – and who would now blame them? They were stormy times. In a hundred years our nation had lived through something like a civil war, a couple of disastrous depressions, two world wars and a murderous sideshow in South Africa, not to mention the tough everyday conditions of a frontier society.

It's not a problem of blame in hindsight, but of now facing a true picture of ourselves. In one part of the essay I wrote:

. . . The thing is, we were all so used to seeing [the violence], that our memories have become defective.

We fail to remember because it was so usual. It was a bit like spitting. Thirty or forty years ago, the gutters, and often quite a bit of the pavement, of Queen Street were splattered with phlegm. People hoiked-up in fusillades. There were notices up on the lamp-posts threatening fines – it took a perfect shot to hit one.

When I mentioned the matter recently I was astonished to be told it was all in my imagination – there was no spitting . . .

Curiously enough, the thing that really got the opposition going was my statement about public spitting.

'You're a bloody liar,' people shouted down the phone. There were no such notices. It didn't happen here. New Zealanders never spat.

But there *were* notices – blue and white enamel plaques stating that you could be fined for the offence were nailed to the lampposts. And the government also ran a poster campaign, with notices plastered all over town, especially in the railway station, the ferry building and at bus stops and the central bus terminal.

There were still quite a few of the enamel plaques to be found in junk shops around the country, but the poster evidence was harder to locate. Eventually, however, it turned up in a book called *A Lovely Day Tomorrow*, by Hamish Keith and Phillip Ridge. On page eight of the book is a reproduction of the poster, issued by the Department of Health. It depicts a huge goobie splattered over a neat office block. Across the poster is a slogan which reads 'Don't Spit!' Underneath is the message, 'It's disgusting and dangerous.' The poster is aimed not at tramps or derelicts, but at a group of well-dressed white-collar workers, shop assistants, suburban housewives and a schoolboy crossing a city street. These are the people who hoiked up their lungs and emptied their sinuses over our footpaths. That's the way things were. And it demonstrates that, in one respect at least, we've changed for the better.

How did I manage to conduct this amateur sociological research, with such authority, so young? Simply by observing, in the way I'd been trained by the writers of the books I devoured endlessly. There were three main places where a boy could observe the regular violence that was the insidious and dominant feature of life in the 1940s and 50s.

The first was in the streets, and it was usually brought about directly by our appalling booze laws. I saw lots of fights around town over the years, sometimes between well-dressed grey-haired men, and several times I witnessed soldiers beating each other up or being bashed with truncheons by military policemen. Fighting in bars, and in the streets after six o'clock, was endemic. After the war, almost every time you passed the Albert Hotel on a Saturday there would be a street brawl, which would be stopped by the forces of the law just before it developed into a riot. It was part of the regular scene.

The second was at school, where hardly a day went by without some poor miscreant being flogged; and the vicious ritualised bullying that took place in the classroom and playground still makes me sick to recollect. I have seen little girls as well as boys strapped at primary school by some huge hulking pervert for no better reason than that the child had exceeded the allowable quota of mistakes in a spelling or arithmetic test.

School was a very dangerous place, especially for a runt like myself. When I returned to Takapuna Primary School, after my stay in the country with Biddy and Mac, I used to keep vocabulary notebooks in which I jotted down any words I came across that I didn't understand. Whenever I had an opportunity later I would look them up in a dictionary and try to learn them off by heart. One day in standard five we had our usual morning rollcall, and when the teacher came to 'Smith,' there was no reply of 'Present, sir.'

'Smith,' the teacher called again. There was still no answer.

'Is Smith absent?' the teacher asked, looking directly at Smith's empty desk. No one answered, so I said, 'Apparently, sir.' It was a word I had only just come across in my reading, looked up, learned to spell and committed to memory. It was a lovely, glittering coin of a word, and here was a chance to use it accurately and helpfully – or so I thought, for I had no knowledge of its insolent possibilities. There was nothing in the dictionary to warn me about its perils.

The next thing I was dragged out in front of the class. There was no explanation sought, and no mercy given. I was strapped so long and viciously that I couldn't write in class for a couple of days. That kind of treatment of a tiny, skinny, bookish boy borders on the psychotic.

And the third place where stupid violence was practised was in the home, where the punishments were severe and premeditated, and carried out entirely without preliminary fair hearings. My brother and I thought our father was a hard man, and we got knocked around at times, but he was an angel compared to some of the dads who came home after work to be greeted straight off by the complaints and accusations laid against the children by their mothers.

UNDER THE BRIDGE & OVER THE MOON

I know, because I used to deliver the *Auckland Star* on an evening paper-round, and I would sometimes arrive home ill and trembling, with the sounds of the terrible beatings being inflicted on the young of Takapuna still ringing in my head. Evenings were the time when so many of the otherwise starch-collared, besuited, betied and behatted pillars of our communities got home and were at last able to take out the festering frustrations of their cramped and hate-ridden lives on someone smaller and weaker than themselves.

A paper-round is the place for a boy to learn what's going on in his neighbourhood. A few years of it and you get an eye and an ear for the cruelty camouflaged by the standard roses and the lace curtains.

It was only a week or so before writing this record that I was talking to an elderly Devonport neighbour of mine about the truth, as we saw it, of the 'good old days' – as some still describe them. She told me a story that she said had warped the whole of her early adult life. At the age of seventeen she thought she would experiment with what it must be like to wear slacks, so she borrowed a pair of her brother's trousers and walked up the street in them. When she returned home from her daring adventure her father took her into her bedroom and beat her black and blue with his belt.

But I am not attempting to generate a kind of contra-myth: that there was endless violence. I am merely observing that there was far too much brutality, and that it was so deeply ingrained in both public and private behaviour that people failed to recognise what was going on. The particular comment that follows from this is that the huge, casual, everyday and unpredictable swings from rage to intense affection led to the many varieties of emotional and moral confusion that my generation suffered from in our attitudes towards each other and ourselves.

Of course there was love – and deep and compassionate love at that – though too often it was delivered to us in parcels, between the violence and wrapped in sentiment.

There was huge love in our family. The times I can connect my father with feelings of absolute admiration and undying love are among the most precious recollections of a lifetime. The best of all these moments would be when I wake woken from sleep sometimes at four o'clock in the morning to find a cup of hot tea being thrust into my hands.

'Get it down quick,' he would whisper so as not to wake the whole household. 'We'll have a boatload of fish before sparrow-fart.'

We would load the wheelbarrow with lines, bait and anchor. It would still be dark, but we'd set off down Rewhiti Avenue for the beach, with me carrying the oars and him pushing the barrow. In no time we'd be dragging our dinghy across the sand and soon we'd be off to our favourite spots, sometimes as far out as the old black buoy.

Then just before sunrise, dawn would bleach the skies, and there would be a moment of perfect stillness when there was no breeze, as if all the effort of the world's breathing in and out was going into the strain of pushing the sun over the summit of Rangitoto. Then the blueness would come and a low molten hump of golden light would spread along the horizon and the next thing it would pump up and form into a blinding bubble then suddenly pop into the sky.

These are the moments when everything that was unexpressed between father and son would fall into place and we would share all the love in our hearts without a word being said. It has taken me more than fifty years to find the words to fashion a poem from such simplicity:

My father lived by the measure
that if you got out on the water by dawn
the fish would queue up for the hook.

It was not just a rule for filling the sack,
there was virtue in it. The pleasure
of sprawling out in the sun, reading a book,

head cradled in the crotch of the bow,
line slung over a toe, foot dangling
over the side, was no way

to earn food. He worked at it. And if
the wind got up and his hands blistered
and he soaked us all, rowing into the spray,

the fish tasted better. It was part of the heartless
perfection of living. Like cleaning the catch
on the beach and tossing the guts

to the gulls. It was their portion, their due.
Except for the livers and roes, which were ours.
We scoffed them for starters with thin cuts

of skinned fillet, fried in butter for precisely
ten seconds, turned briefly, then tipped out
on hot toast. One more ritual that brought

UNDER THE BRIDGE & OVER THE MOON

luck and protection. With fish, you never defied
the way things ought to be done –
the sea was no place for free thought,

break the code and you're dead. I cannot
escape this conditioning. Nor forget how,
back at home, the old man would pour

a stiff slug of madeira to get the blood
moving again. That such a moderate drinker
could tipple that muck in the raw

of the morning shall always amaze me.
Perhaps it was something he worked at,
like the virtue of fishing – a recompense

for obeying the rules. No treat in itself,
but good in the afterglow. Our fathers exist
to uphold the law, not to make sense.

32: Defence mechanisms

If there is one person who stands out in a shining light during those
dark years it is my elder sister Ann. From the age of ten, while she
was still at primary school, she took over the running of the whole
household.

She cooked, cleaned and bossed the rest of us about, and somehow
stopped us from lapsing into lassitude or total anarchy. We all had a list
of jobs that had to be done: my father's evening meal was always ready
when he came home from work, the chooks were fed, the beds were
made, and the dishes were only occasionally stacked overnight in the
sink. She led by example. It was a heroic response from a little girl.

She was also my protector and defender against the bullies and their
cowardly hangers-on who roamed Takapuna in morose, jeering gangs.
Unfairness roused Ann to fury, so when one day she looked out from a
front window of our house and saw that one of the terrors of our
neighbourhood, egged on by his snivelling cohorts, had me bailed up in

the street and was giving me the treatment, she flew outside, grabbed the boy, flung him to the ground and sat on him, pounding the wind out of him with her bum.

The bully went crimson in the face, then burst out crying and moaning for mercy. I had no further trouble from him for a full year, and when he did eventually catch me on my own again and began the finger-jabbing ritual that was the usual preliminary to a bashing, I just grinned at him and asked how he'd like to be sat on again by my big sister. The boy looked at me in horror, then ran for it. His humiliation was a joy to see: he was frightened of girls.

My father tried to do something more manly and practical about my helplessness. Because I was so thin and tiny he had me out on the back lawn in boxing gloves, teaching me how to lead with your left and throw a right. He also tried to get me to go to the local gym and take lessons from the kindly old ex-pro who gave boxing lessons there.

My first night was a revelation. All the local bullies were there refining their skills, thumping each other and storing up some painful information that I'd be lucky not to learn later on the streets or in the playground. It seemed nonsense to me that in addition to the normal hazards of life I should also volunteer to come to this place of agony and take an extra weekly working over.

There was a dangerous side to my father's ambitions for me. Paying for me to become a human punch-bag was nuts. I told the ex-pro that I wasn't going to come here and fight and no one was going to make me. Of course my father and I had an argument about it, and I got the usual threats and exhortations – 'manliness' was the word that cropped up over and over again – but the ex-pro said to me, 'You stick to your guns, sonny.' And he said to my father, 'He's all right. He's a stubborn bugger.' So I was allowed to get away with my refusal. I didn't appreciate it at the time, but his words were a fair example of what I later came to recognise as understated Kiwi male praise. They worked the trick.

I also enjoyed a brief induction into the local scout troop – until my big mouth got me into trouble. The scoutmaster, and the Akela of the Takapuna cubs, was a decent good old man who was admired throughout the scout movement. He strived hard and sincerely to encourage us to become better human beings; and after all he did have a pretty effective inducement to offer us – getting togged up in fancy dress.

There was something heroic and glorious about the gear we were entitled to wear: the peaked hat, the blue scarf with the single gold star and the shell toggle, the khaki shirt with the sleeve flash, the badges for passing tests, the green tags that hung from the elastic garters that kept your socks up to a regulation hand's width below the knee, and there was always the glowering wolf's head buckle on the leather belt. It made a boy feel he was accepted, glamorous and worthwhile.

However, what soon got on my goat was the constant indoctrination. I couldn't stand the simple-minded clammy Jesus-stories that were drilled into us every time we sat around in a circle. It was like Sunday school with time off for lessons in tying reef knots blindfolded. The only thing missing was an evangelist card for good attendance. I'd been impressed by all that when I'd listened to the mad-eyed young woman in my two years at Cambridge, but I felt now that I'd grown out of it. The simpering Jesus that Akela was gumming on about was the same one who'd been in too much of a trance to respond in the moonlight to my entreaties when Moya and Sheila had paid their sudden visit to Biddy. After one too many of these tacky and sanctimonious sessions with the scouts I began to refer to the movement as the Hitler Youth.

It was a joke that I can now see it would still be a mistake to crack, but at the end of the war it was particularly offensive. Word got around. Nobody thought it funny, and though I was not actually drummed out, the scouts and I agreed to part company. I never again found uniforms attractive. They altered people in ways that I found difficult to come to terms with. Even one of the most decent old men in Takapuna somehow became a single-minded martinet and weirdly worrying religious maniac when he slipped into his scout gear.

At secondary school I made the same discovery. A year after the war's end, and with the army changing back into civilian clothes, the boys had to turn up to school every Wednesday in military uniform. This was not made out of lightweight material suitable for the Auckland climate, but of heavy, prickly serge with polished brass buttons. We called them 'sandpaper suits' and every summer several little boys would faint in this ridiculous outfit while standing at attention on parade.

Wednesday morning classes were made intolerable by the discomfort of wearing the uniform, so that we were dressed and ready to devote the whole afternoon to being drilled and instructed in the arts of warfare by teachers who changed absurdly from being mere cane-happy boy-hating brutes into wild-eyed fantasists and tyrants of the King's Regulations. We were made to sign oaths of allegiance, and one lunatic of a teacher in a make-believe uniform warned us that from now on we had to realise we were soldiers and any of us could be court-martialled and shot by firing squad.

After a year of that I'd had enough, so when I finished my stint in the third form I went to the headmaster and told him that I was not going to come to school in uniform any more. This was entirely against my father's urging. Despite his left-wing politics, his argument was the same as the one he'd used to try to get me to have my head knocked off once a week at the gym: military drill was 'manly' and you never knew when the training would come in useful.

But when it came to the point, and he saw that I was going to persist stubbornly in refusing to dress up, my father reluctantly sided with me. He recited to me the question that the headmaster would inevitably put: What would you do if an enemy soldier was trying to rape your sister? And he taught me the Lytton Strachey reply, which was the question's only devastating answer: 'I'd try to get between them, sir.'

The question, as it so happened, was not put to me straight off and in the exact manner that my father had anticipated. First of all the headmaster asked me in a kindly and understanding way if my father had coached me in my rebellious attitude, and I told him truthfully that my father was actually against it and there had been plenty of soldiers in my family. Well, he then asked, have you become a pacifist? No, I replied, I was most definitely not a pacifist. I just wasn't going to come to school ever again in a silly uniform and be bossed around by people I thought had gone crazy.

The headmaster looked at me severely and I thought for a moment I was running pretty close to getting six of the best. Then he asked the question I had been waiting for. Except that instead of asking what I would do if my sister was about to be raped, he mentioned my mother, so I didn't use the answer I had rehearsed, but simply said, 'I haven't got one. I haven't got a mother.'

That did it. The headmaster must have imagined that he'd made some sort of frightful gaffe, for the effect of my reply was extraordinary. These were still the days when families had married mothers and fathers at their heads, before the social wreckers offered financial bribes to young women to deliberately and actively smash, in one generation, the mutually responsible relationships that human society had been developing over several thousand years; so the headmaster looked away and pretended to have a fit of coughing. When he recovered, his face was still red and he told me he'd never been presented with a case like

UNDER THE BRIDGE & OVER THE MOON

this before, and that in the circumstances he really couldn't see why an exception could not be made to accommodate me.

The outcome of this interview was that I was told to come to school in my normal school uniform (rolled-up sleeves, open-necked shirt, roman sandals) so long as I kept myself out of sight on the rifle range at the back of the school. This turned out not to be a punishment and disgrace, but one of the most delightful perks the school could offer a boy, for it meant that every week I helped one of the few sane masters hand out the rifles and ammunition, and did my careful best to stop some of the more overexcitable boys in military uniform from shooting each other or themselves.

It was also my responsibility to count up and record meticulously every boy's success at scoring bulls and for grouping on a cardboard target. And the extra reward was that every time there was a spare butt available I could indulge in a bit of private target practice. Training week after week like this for the next four years meant that I became the best shot at the school, though I could never qualify for the silver cup because it had to go to a boy in the cadet corps.

When my brother enrolled at the same school two years later, I told him not to turn out for the first parade when uniforms were handed out, but to come up to the range and be my assistant. It was a brilliant piece of nepotism. The master merely nodded and grinned when I explained that Mit was my brother and that he was eager to help us with our onerous duties. No further word was necessary; it was simply understood that my brother enjoyed the same position of privilege that I did.

It is one of those mysteries of life, to which you can only respond with a shrug and a smile, that the only boy who had the initiative to follow our example was a third former who had watched my brother's magical uniformless elevation to the delights of the rifle range.

He wasn't prepared to just stand by and envy us, but decided to wander up to the range one day and challenge us directly. He approached us in the ammo shed and said, without any beating about, that he knew that we were brothers, and he wasn't silly because he could see only too plainly that we were working a racket, and he wanted his fair and rightful share of it. My brother and I told him to bugger off smartly and warned him he was going the right way to earn himself a blood-nose, but he was a persistent single-minded boy and was prepared to make a great nuisance of himself.

The situation could have become hilarious. My brother had never sought the headmaster's permission for his privileges and now I could imagine all the boys in the school taking it into their minds one by one to join me up on the rifle range, until there was no cadet corps left. Something had to be done to stop the rot. So I said to the boy that it would be all right for him not to wear the uniform and to come up to the range, but that he had to understand that there was a definite pecking order. My brother and I had first crack at all the spare shooting and he could have whatever was left over.

Then I went to the master in charge and said that the work seemed to be getting heavier and more complicated, what with the new and neater and more reliable way I was copying down the scores, but that luckily I now had an extra assistant, so everything would go on just as normal. The master was a bit tricky to deal with at first, but since he taught science and not humanities, he had the unadulterated imagination and the good humour to comprehend the cool convoluted beauty of my statement. He needed only a little further private thought, then he simply accepted the new arrangement in silence, and soon we all got on very well.

The clever intruder's name was Bill, but my brother and I called him Cream Puff, because of his devotion to the goodies sold in the tuck shop. When I left school I forgot all about Bill until about thirty years later, when I met him again up at my brother's farm, and learnt that he and my brother had become married to two sisters.

33: FOOTY, FISHING & SHOOTING

The lazy dreamlike quality of the mid 1940s reflected itself in my secondary school record. I was an indifferent scholar, because I was lazy, dreamy one.

The headmaster, whose reaction to my intransigence over the matter of the uniform showed that he was a decent high-principled man, was near retiring age and the school was in a temporary downturn after its high-flying days of the 1930s and early 40s.

The pattern of general slackness showed up not only in our poor intellectual efforts but even on the sports fields. The soccer team I eventually joined, after getting tired of having my nose smashed (three times in all) playing rugby, was almost glorious in its ineptitude. The group of boys I played with made it a point of flagrant style and inverse arrogance to be the worst in the schools competition, and since I also played club soccer for the North Shore club I knew only too well what was going on.

We used to see how hard we could throw ourselves at the ball and still come out losers. It was also a matter of pride that in all the years we played as a team we never won a match – except once, when one truly vulgar, bad-sport school included in their team some older yobbos who had left school, and we promptly had them disqualified on the grounds that that we could lose well enough ourselves without anyone having to bring in reinforcements.

The trouble was that we had one brilliant player, and that presented us with a moral problem. My friend Duncan McCormack was a wing in what I came to learn (when I regularly watched Tottenham Hotspur and Chelsea in London) was the elegant old Corinthian tradition.

A Corinthian wing would trap a long floated pass on the run, dribble the ball down the touch-line at speed, pass the halfback with a body swerve, then take the ball almost to the corner flag, cut inside the fullback with a jinky one-two, and either place the ball in the net from an acute angle or drop it at the feet of the centre-forward as he steamed towards the goalmouth.

Well, that was the general idea. But what always happened with us was that we fooled about and forgot about the opposition while we tackled each other ferociously for the ball and scored own-goals and created an absolute shambles. It was unfair on Duncan and a great burden to us. He was never to experience the pleasure of playing for a winning team, not even when he was selected for the Auckland schoolboy reps.

Just before he was to turn out in the Auckland colours we were playing our usual anarchist interpretation of the game on the Domain, just below the War Memorial Museum, when the ball accidentally flew off someone's boot, up in the air in a perfect arc towards our single ace player. Duncan trapped the ball and moved forward, all with one graceful flick of the boot – except that the heavy leather ball landed in a patch of mud and just stuck there. His foot stayed behind the ball while his body headed for goal.

The sickening sound of his leg breaking was as loud as the crack of a gun or the bang a tree makes as it begins to crash to the ground. The report brought every game to a standstill. It echoed right across the Domain.

Duncan and I had a friendly rivalry as fishermen, and after a good weekend we'd come to school and compare exaggerated accounts of the hauls we'd made. He lived at Milford and boasted that the best fishing grounds were off the beach there, while I maintained that nothing could beat Takapuna beach when it came to prize snapper. Eventually we agreed to put the matter to the test. He would come out with me off Takapuna one day after school and I'd go out with him off Milford later in the week.

The first day of this contest arrived and we dashed back to my place on our bikes, then raced down to the beach where that morning I'd got the dinghy ready. We pushed off, rowed out about half a mile and dropped the pick, then threw out our handlines. As soon as the sinkers hit bottom our baits were hit by big-sized snapper and soon we were pulling them in by the dozen. Almost every time we baited our hooks we'd have more fish. The snapper were nearly up to our knees. Then we realised we were almost sinking – we had only two or three inches of freeboard. Slowly and carefully we hauled in the anchor. Then we rowed for shore, with Duncan gently pulling on the oars while I leaned forward on them to help with a gentle push.

A small breeze had got up and every now and again a wave would lap over the gunwales and threaten catastrophe. It took us an age to get back, and we ended up on St Leonard's beach, then had to haul the dinghy by its painter along the shallows and around the King and Queen rocks back to Takapuna.

A crowd gathered, so we started scaling and gutting our catch, and flogging off the fish at one and sixpence each (fifteen cents). But we were so exhausted that we had to give that up. We lowered the price to a bob each and by nightfall we had over four pounds (eight dollars) in our pockets. It was a small fortune. We counted eighty-four snapper altogether. And there was no need for a return match at Milford. Duncan told me before he biked home that he had thought up till then that all my Takapuna fishing tales were bullshit, but he now had to agree: Milford wasn't in the same competition.

Of course, it was all a fluke, but how could I possibly own up to that? What relieved me more than anything was that we hadn't canned

UNDER THE BRIDGE & OVER THE MOON

out and lost the whole boatload. Not to mention an ignominious swim back to the beach. We had been excessively greedy and competitive and we were bloody lucky on more than one count.

Duncan and I were also friends in a small group of 'aesthetes'. It was a word we liked to wave about occasionally to outrage our contemporaries, even though we were far too coarse, tongue-tied and gawky ever to have been able to defend ourselves against serious challenge or ridicule. As I recall it, we were given the word by one of the most extraordinary schoolboys I ever ran into. He was a comical freckled asthmatic with the fine bones and pointed features of an elf, and though he was a poor student he was well read in what one of our English masters termed 'decadent' literature – by which he meant not just the unmentionable Oscar Wilde and the depraved Algernon Charles Swinburne, but everything disgustingly French, from Rabelais to Proust.

His parents lived in rather grand though seedy circumstances, and their domestic arrangements were mysterious, so the boy was far more socially advanced than we were. On the rare and delicious occasions when he would invite us to his home, he would offer us a selection of records that included Gigli, Galli-Curci and Caruso, played on a monster wind-up gramophone. There was also a complete *Scheherazade*, which he told us was the finest piece of music ever written, and we were only too happy to echo the opinion as though it was our own.

While we stood about in our first pairs of long trousers, smoking tailormades and gazing from his verandah at the lights reflecting across Auckland harbour, listening to Rimsky-Korsakov played over and over again, he would mix us cocktails from his parents' liquor cabinet, each an individual creation to fit his interpretation of our personalities. We would pass these absurd and sometimes vile concoctions around and taste them thoughtfully and always agree that yes, he had summed up so-and-so's character and disposition to a T.

It all makes me laugh to remember, but at the time I felt deeply honoured to have a potion of high-octane liqueurs mixed specially to suit me. Looking back on it now, I'd say that my first cocktail and my first pair of long trousers were like passports that instantly admitted me across an invisible border from one state of identity to another. With a bizarre drink in my hand and with my skinny legs hidden from sight I felt the first buzz of what it was going to be like to be a grown-up. I owe that strange little elfin boy a huge debt of gratitude.

I also owe him thanks for a brilliant memory that stands out from the dreary run of most of my schooling. One day we were lying about talking about the hell of having to go to school and being forced to suffer the warped and vicious bullying that was practised on us by our masters, when one of our number piped up that he would like to shoot one of the creepier sadists on the staff. The next day our sophisticated friend and mentor drew us aside in the playground and asked the boy if a shooting still seemed desirable.

'Bloody oath,' came the reply from the young would-be aesthete.

'Well, here's your gun, dear boy,' said the other and produced from a silk handkerchief a gleaming .22 lady's-handbag automatic complete with ammunition.

It was a moment of stunning theatricality. We all took turns to hold and inspect the little handgun, then it was given back. The silk handkerchief was folded carefully around the butt and stubby barrel. There was to be no shooting after all, it seemed.

34: MIRACLES

Under Ann's unflagging leadership I somehow advanced through my later childhood and even survived some unimaginative attempts to kill myself by the usual means, including being knocked off my pushbike by a car and getting hooked up in the mains electricity.

Then came the perfect summer of the great poliomyelitis scare. I was fourteen and the weediest midget in 5A Boys. I was so small that people kept mistaking me for a third former. My younger sister was taller and heavier than I was. My little brother was a giant compared with me. Many of the boys in my form were twice my weight. Duncan McCormack's mother was so appalled at the sight of me that she had 'borrowed' me for a couple of months during the previous year in order to hand-feed me and compel me to grow. Every day she would stuff me full of porridge and eggs at breakfast, and keep ramming my gullet till evening with plates of nourishing fattening broadening widening and elongating fuel. But she had to give up. My body just wouldn't respond. I was destined to be one the short-arses of this world.

But when polio struck in our School Certificate year, suddenly two miracles occurred. The first was – as if in answer to my wildest dreams – there was no school. For the whole of the first term the doors remained closed. The teachers got busy on stencils and Gestetners, and they distributed what they called 'assignments' (class notes and projects, complete with heaps and heaps of homework) to our letterboxes, so that everyone could keep up with the syllabus.

I used to conceal myself behind the sunporch curtains and slyly watch the teachers come and go, and when I'd savoured the pleasure of seeing them disappear, I'd go out and fetch each special delivery and file it away under my bed where I wouldn't be outraged by having to look at it ever again. What was the point of being given time off school and spoiling it with work that no one could force you to do? I expected to get into big trouble if the teachers got hold of me eventually, but in the meantime there was always the delirious possibility that the polio scare might never go away and the schools would have to stay shut forever.

I had a huge pile of books to read for private enjoyment and instruction, and there was our wonderful beach just down at the bottom of the road (it was almost deserted, for we were not supposed to go near the sea, which was said to be full of dangerous germs), and there were fish to be caught and rock oysters to be cracked off the rocks at low tide and eaten raw (and illegally) by the dozen. The months certainly weren't wasted. I was reading and enjoying myself flat out all day, every day. It was just that I didn't have enough time left over to do schoolwork.

And as if that wasn't paradise enough, I was blest with a second miracle. I remember going to bed one evening and feeling a strange aching sensation in my limbs. Holy hell, I thought at first, I've got bloody polio.

However, I didn't feel sick or dizzy, so I went off to sleep as usual. The next night, and the one after that, I felt the same odd and uncomfortable sensation. Then I realised what must be happening. Just when everyone, including myself, had given up all hope, I had started to grow.

And not just grow, but sprout, like bamboo. I swear I could sometimes hear my body clicking and creaking at night. Going to bed was like lying on a rack. I was being stretched bone by bone and sinew by sinew.

And during the day it was just as bad. When I ran down the beach to go for yet another banned swim, I kept on stumbling and tripping over my own legs.

There is no object in nature as unlovely as an adolescent boy. Girls seem to have a natural sense of self-possession and poise to cope with budding breasts and spreading hips. But boys become ungainly and smelly, and their treacherous vocal chords threaten to turn every remark into a squawk of self-parody.

As if it wasn't a bad enough blow to suffer such a serious dose of adolescence all in a few weeks, the summer ended, the polio scare receded and the schools reopened. I returned to my studies in a new set of clothes, two or three sizes larger, well aware that even if this did manage to impress anyone (it didn't), I was likely to get a flogging from every resentful master whose best efforts to encourage me to answer their assignments had been entirely ignored.

In the event, everyone was too busy coping with post-closure chaos to care. I was delighted to discover that I was simply going to be ignored and I settled down to enjoy the rest of the year fooling about and reading while my body got on with the business of growing. School Certificate could wait till the following year so far as I was concerned.

However, my father thought differently – he had paid the exam fee, and insisted that the money shouldn't be wasted – so I decided the best thing to do was pretend to be sitting the exams, then just slip off to the beach and go fishing.

I had just made this decision when an odd thing happened. I was sitting in class a week before the first paper when a master announced that work was finished for the year and that from now on it was all a foregone conclusion: those who would pass were certain to do so and those who would fail could do nothing about it.

Promptly, one of the class sycophants raised his hand and said, 'Please sir, does that mean you already know who will pass and who will fail?'

'Yes,' the master said. 'I could tell you who will pass and who won't with absolute certainty.'

Hands popped up everywhere. 'Please sir, tell us,' the boys begged.

If the master had been a small bird – say, a hedge sparrow – he would have fluffed out his feathers with pride. No, no, he chirped happily, he couldn't possibly . . .

The boys wagged their hands at him and pleaded and wheedled. Then the master held up both arms as if in surrender and said, 'I won't tell you who will pass. That is quite unnecessary, for those boys already know they will. But I'll tell you who will most definitely fail . . .'

He pointed directly at me. 'Stand up, boy,' he shouted.

I shuffled upright.

'This boy did not return a single assignment. Since school reopened he has not done a tap of work. How he came to be in an A form at all I've no idea. He may as well leave school now. He is the most certain failure I've ever known in my whole teaching career . . .'

I think he must have surprised himself with his own vehemence. He happened to be absolutely right in everything he said, but he must have realised he'd lost some dignity by allowing himself to be caught off guard by anger when he should have been basking in the craven adulation of his toadies. He stopped in a fluster and refused to be cajoled into further disclosures.

I sat down and looked back at him with contempt. You bastard, I thought, just for that I'll show you. I'll pass your stupid bloody exam.

By borrowing classmates' notes and exercise books I mugged up enough in a few days to scrape through with marks to spare. I suppose I have mostly to thank a teacher called Peter Kania, who had somehow managed to force enough mathematics past the barrier of my excessive indolence to gain me a pass in the one subject that could have failed me, but without the incentive of that other master's perfectly disgraceful classroom antics, I'd never have bothered at all.

More than anything, I suppose, it shows what a contrary, prickly and wilful little freak I was becoming. And it had a sequel that can only make me shake my head in wonder. The experience gave me such a stir-up that I worked immoderately the following year and disgraced myself by coming top of the first-year sixth form. It was a time-wasting academic overexertion that caused much embarrassment at school and at home. I readjusted my sights and decided never to make the same mistake again.

The notion was only a vague one at the time, but I was already setting my aims on never becoming an academic or a schoolteacher. Whatever I did, however, it had to have something to do with the written word. Secretly I began to wonder if I just might have a poem or two, or perhaps even a book, inside me . . .

35: MARJORIE & AFTER

We had several housekeepers who were hired from time to time to try to organise the household. I have only a vague recollection of them, for they were mostly shadowy distracted souls. Apart from one ferociously capable Scotswoman, and a gifted Wellington woman who pretended to be a Canadian and was therefore eventually bawled out as a liar by my father, who had strict notions about such things, the only consistent qualification they seemed to have was that they were hopelessly disorganised and sometimes downright dirty. They obviously wanted the job only because they had already failed at everything else. They never lasted and we children became expert at subtle subversions that would help them decide to leave. Ann, with Carole's support, would simply take over the job again – capably and without complaint.

Then the amazing Marjorie came along. She and my father fell in love, married and suddenly we had a mother again.

Marjorie had run the famous Delicious Sponges shops in Queen Street and Karangahape Road, so she was a great manager as well as cook. My brother and I used to boast that her sponge cakes were so feathery that if a door was opened when they were cooling on a wire rack, the slightest puff of wind would pick them up, and it was our job to stand guard and if necessary chase them around the kitchen with hammers, and nail them to the walls before they floated out of the windows and were lost forever.

Four children, trained and skilled in sabotaging all previous adult interventions in our household, must have been a formidable challenge, but Marjorie took us on and proved to be one of the most extraordinary women who has ever drawn breath. She was – and still is – utterly lovely.

Suddenly life began to get better for all of us. My brother and I became almost maniacal junior contractors and entrepreneurs. We delivered newspapers, mowed old ladies' lawns, dug gardens, flogged off surplus eggs and vegetables from our backyard (unbeknown to our father), went fishing out in the channel and sold snapper, organised our own paper collections and bottle drives – in fact, we worked all the hours we were not forced to spend in the prison of secondary school.

We used to chuck all the money we jointly and severally earned into a single bag in our bedroom wardrobe and whenever we decided to go over the harbour to town and have a good time, or perhaps make a special purchase or just stroll along to see the flicks at the Gaiety cinema in Takapuna, we would put our fists into the bag and draw out whatever we needed. No account was kept and the money was never shared out in proportion to our earnings. Yet the bag never emptied. Sometimes one of us would have an especially profitable week, but that made no difference. We tossed in whatever we got and that entitled us to equal rights over the contents.

Years afterwards, as a matter of curiosity only, I asked my brother if he had ever slipped into the wardrobe in secret and tallied up the money or checked what was going in and coming out. Never ever, he replied. Had I?

Not once, I said. And we looked into each other's eyes and knew it was true. And we also knew that that was the reason why the bag was bottomless – why there was always money in it. If either of us had ever given in to greed or suspicion the only thing we'd have found in the bag would have been moths.

All this coming together intimately and effectively as a family was probably due to the way that Marjorie and my father provided a stable and loving centre to our lives, but it was also coincidentally the brief calm prelude to our growing out of childhood and going our different ways.

My sisters were soon to marry friends of mine – Ron Fairley was taken care of by Ann, and Graeme Blair was accounted for by Carole. My brother was to go into his own business before marrying his wife Jocelyn and becoming the very good farmer that his visits to the little country school and his natural horsemanship had promised. And I spent some time temporarily at university, largely because that was a compromise I eventually hammered out with my father. As my last year at secondary school came to an end there were regular quarrels between us. He wanted to see me become academically qualified, while my two ambitions were to go to sea or to enrol at art school.

I'm sure I would have enjoyed both experiences, and sometimes wonder what would have happened if I'd done so, but I didn't want to do either strongly enough to hold out against the alternative arguments. I could have simply gone my own way if I'd really wanted to, for in those days it was easy to pursue whatever vague choices you felt like making. Holiday jobs at the freezing works and woolstores, and several stints as a tally clerk on the wharves and later in the goods yard of the railways, provided me with the wherewithal to do whatever I liked.

As it happened, I'm glad I took my father's advice. University turned out to be everything I didn't expect. It was a place of liberation, though often in contradictory ways. It was also not just a place of learning, but for those who took the trouble it gave a useful crash course in sifting through our civilisation's accumulated clutter of facts, concepts and opinions, and learning how each of these can so easily be mistaken for the other. And it offered *style*, which was a quality I had never run into before, except perhaps in the exceptional and precocious instance of the elfin boy who played *Scheherazade* and brought a handgun to school wrapped in a silk handkerchief – though the style to be gained from a university is a great deal more subtle than that, and almost as instantly detectable.

It's not a snobbish thing (though it can be made to seem so), for I'm not using the word with any implication of elegance or superiority, but simply in its sense of distinctiveness – the 'style' I am referring to derives directly from practical habits of formal discipline, which allow those who have learnt from their training to take shortcuts and make mental leaps with confidence. A person such as Mac, my maternal grandfather – for all his lifelong hunger for knowledge, the remarkable range of his reading and the retentive brilliance of his mind – nearly always ends up on a cracker-barrel. It was a situation that he was well aware of himself, with a terrible self-disparaging pain. Even a year or two at a university for anyone with average brains is enough to give those drives and abilities a convincing and confident shape, however wrongly directed they may be.

I thank the institution for all those things, and it was not its fault that it didn't also make a good scholar out of me. I sat some exams and I have a feeling that I passed most of them, though a stubborn refusal to prepare for any test or paper until the night before I sat it made the process pretty chancy.

But more than that I gained the gift of several lifelong friendships and a gradual insight into the condition that almost two decades of voracious reading had landed me in – there was going to be no release from the world of writing. I was stuck there between covers. Not so much hooked as booked.

The dark side to university was also unexpected – and distressing. The year I enrolled was a turning point in our history. It was 1951, and when I turned up for my first lectures the great fight to the finish between the government and wharfies had just started. Their confrontation is now usually referred to as the 1951 Waterfront Dispute, though at the time it was called a strike or lockout – depending, of course, which side you were on.

It was certainly described as a lockout in our house, for there was no doubt in our minds what the truth of the matter was. My father had gone to work as a seagull on the wharf, where his well-known radical views and his unusual latent abilities as a union organiser (he became a key figure in founding that most unlikely of militant organisations, an insurance clerks' and agents' union) meant that in no time at all he became a fully fledged member of the union.

The dispute was a disgraceful episode, quite as violently traumatic and just as wickedly stupid as the row over the Springbok tour in 1981. But the levels of public enforcement and barefaced hypocrisy that went along with the 1951 dispute were far worse, and something that even Prime Minister Muldoon never dared attempt.

As the rights and wrongs of working conditions on the wharves and the true causes of conflict in 1951 pass into historical debate and left-wing myth, the one thing we should never distance our minds from is that Sid Holland, our National Party prime minister at the time, ruled this country for five months of the bitterest civil strife it had experienced in almost one hundred years, without summoning Parliament. Not once did he call for a compulsory conference between the two sides. And, in the greatest executive violation ever perpetrated by a New Zealand government on its citizens, he suspended a vast range of our civil liberties, including even the right to hold political meetings to discuss the rights and wrongs of the issues – and transformed our freedoms into crimes against the state – by a set of Emergency Regulations that ironically the previous Labour Government had passed at the outbreak of war in 1939 and never repealed.

I have seen enough of politics and politicians in my lifetime to know that flexible common sense and practical benevolence achieve far more than all the grand inhuman designs of do-gooders and dogmatists, but no society can ever work when the freedom to blow a raspberry at its rulers is taken away.

The one thing I could never get over was a meeting held in the university hall at the height of the dispute, to debate the one aspect of the dispute that we could talk about openly without getting arrested, put on trial and either fined heavily or imprisoned: the merits of the Emergency Regulations themselves.

About five hundred students attended, which was an extraordinary turnout, given the Cold War neuroses of the times and the level of public anxiety over appearing at what could have looked like a protest rally. It may seem difficult to believe, but in 1951 there were seriously disturbed youths prowling about the university checking out their fellow students, asking questions about their politics and stealing posters on club noticeboards and taking down lists of names, probably to end up on some secret service file.

In my innocence I believed that everyone would condemn the Emergency Regulations; but the students voted a massive nine-to-one in favour of them. I listened to them in amazement. They didn't want to hear the other side of the story, or even whether there might be one. They actually wanted their rulers to take away their right of assembly, their liberty of discussion, their freedom to be given the facts and their choice to think for themselves. Their arguments were shit-scared, spineless and insane. If they hadn't been so appalling they could have come straight out of *Alice in Wonderland*. The gobbledegook they chanted ran like this: the Communists want to take away our freedoms, the wharfies are the same as Communists, therefore it's a perfectly legitimate tactic for our own government to take our freedoms away in order to defeat those who intend to take away our freedoms. And this was God's Own Country, and this was a university?

The experience has convinced me that in any society only ten percent of the population has any notion of democracy and is willing actively to see that our rights and freedoms are preserved in any circumstances. That's all the numbers there ever are to defend our liberties – and they cover the whole spectrum from left to right, excepting the extremes (though in 1951 the representatives of the old Conservative–Liberal right were notably and unusually silent).

But what most astonished me – as I watched the hands of the simpering gobshites tossing and jerking in the air to vote against the civil liberties that had been won for them down the centuries, in the face of imprisonment, torture and death – was that this was not a crowd of hoons, wowsers or rednecks: this was happening in an institution that was supposed to cultivate unfettered minds. Here, at the centre of liberal enlightenment, were our future teachers and leaders bending over with no more backbone than a banana to offer their collective arse to the boots of the most crass lineup of nitwits that has ever held public office in this country.

36: SOMERVELL'S

The reason I bothered to stay on at university for a brief time after the shock of that experience was that it was impossible not to love the place. It offered a unique opportunity to enjoy feeling exceptional and behaving outrageously. And if there had not been those two inducements, I still would have loved the place for no better reason than that I enjoyed the company of a collection of book-swapping, poetry-spouting, word-intoxicated rebels, who included my friend from school, Duncan McCormack, and new friends such as Carl Freeman and Maurice Shadbolt, not to mention a fair sprinkling of mavericks, poseurs, Bohemians and left-wing fascists – the kind of people who were a mirror reflection of the kids who'd packed out the university hall to demonstrate their contempt for civil liberty, except that this lot presented their arses to the boot of Joe Stalin.

The Communists were far fewer around town than the papers led us to believe; but that was part of the strength they wielded, even if it was mostly wish-fulfilment. Everyone, from the newspapers to the government, painted them as powerful – after all, our rulers and leaders would have looked a bit silly if they'd admitted that they were battling bogeymen. Yet the fact of the matter was that there were only ever a few hundred Communists around the whole country, and many of these were in out-of-the-way coalmining places such as Huntly and the West Coast. In addition, it was probable that a fair percentage of the few who had to be reckoned with in the main centres were actually spies and informers on each other. It became a case of the Communists happily assuming the appearance of the menace they were made out to be. It must have made them glow.

I knew several Communists and enjoyed their stimulating company. They appeared to me much as Doris Lessing describes them in her autobiography *Under My Skin*. Most of them were highly intelligent, well motivated and often talented people, and some had a taste for a good time plus a wicked sense of humour. The only thing wrong with them was that at any mention of Russia a shutter dropped over their eyes. Russian communism was no subject for criticism and certainly not one for jokes. It was no good arguing with them about it; they were beyond reach.

I went once with a dozen or so other students, out of curiosity, to their headquarters in St Kevin's Arcade in Karangahape Road, but never repeated the experience. The great Comrade Hugh McLeod was in the chair, yet instead of being pleased to have an opportunity to address so many fresh young faces delivered to him in one haul from the university, our appearance seemed to upset his liver. Several of us would have been wearing tartan shirts and handknitted woollen ties, which was pretty daring for those days, so I suppose instinctively he summed us up as nothing more than a future source of insubordination, deviation and cosmopolitanism.

Whatever it was that got him going, he launched straight into a laborious slogan-loaded tirade about the inevitable victory of the working class (because Karl Marx had proved this 'scientifically' and 'dialectically') and how the intelligentsia (which meant us) might assist in this 'historical' process, but what we needed was a hell of a lot of criticism and self-criticism, which only the Party could provide, but that in any case we were not to think of ourselves as the genuine article in the vanguard of the struggle because we merely handled ideas not the means of production. Besides being drivel, it was the drippiest bit of slow-tap torture I'd ever heard put into spoken words, and I think all of us, but one, came away not only unpersuaded but put off for life. The one exception was a very amiable and clever person who I can only think had been got at and converted sometime earlier.

Our radicalism instead took the form of an anarchic bohemianism centred on Somervell's coffee bar in Queen Street, where on most evenings we took over the cubicles at the back of the premises and drank real coffee, which was served in a proper cup with a saucer, on which was perched a small pot of thick yellow cream.

Bill Wilson and the Group Architects were part of a wider circle that frequented the place, along with a long line of jolly argumentative luminaries such as the typographer and printer Bob Lowry, the landscape gardener and anarchist Odo Strewe, the future union president and

UNDER THE BRIDGE & OVER THE MOON

cabinet minister Eddy Isbey and the painter Denis Knight Turner, and occasionally the poets Allen Curnow and A. R. D. Fairburn, and Ted Middleton the short-story writer. Also joining in the fun were the sculptor Tony Stones, the writers Jean Watson and Maurice Shadbolt, the future editor of *Landfall* and *Islands* Robin Dudding, Frank Finan the glass artist, Nigel Cook the architect and Norman Wong, who was simply his inimitable self.

I cannot recall those evenings without smiling. Somervell's was the place you went to after drinking a skinful of draught, or, if you were feeling rich, a few quart bottles of Waikato XXXX or Pilsener Lager (it had to be one extreme or the other) – usually at the Queen's Ferry (where Ian Middleton could always be found) or the Occidental in Vulcan Lane. Sometimes, however, you would call in after you'd had a meal at the Golden Dragon in Grey's Avenue. The Dragon offered generous half-orders of chop suey or chow mein, for one and ninepence (less than twenty cents), and you supplemented this with a huge stack of free 'blotting paper', which was buttered bread you dipped in soya sauce and scoffed to help mop up the beer till the main course arrived.

Queen Street (and the tiny network of streets that ran off it) was very much the hub of Auckland in those days. Nearly all the tramlines converged like the spokes of a bicycle wheel on the Central Post Office. To get from one side of town to the other meant first a trip to the centre then out again. So, when you'd been to the Queen's Ferry, and followed that with a visit to Somervell's or the Golden Dragon, you'd walk up to the likeliest bedsitter in Grafton Road or you'd catch a tram out to someone's flatlet in Parnell or Mt Eden – always clutching paper-bag parcels of quart bottles of beer.

On Friday or Saturday nights there was inevitably the prospect of a party – at Bob Lowry's place on the slopes of Mt Eden, or perhaps at Odo Strewe's, on the bus route out towards Henderson.

The reason for all this dashing about town every evening – visiting, drinking, declaiming, endlessly arguing and partying – was the six-o'clock swill.

Just about every shop and office closed at five or half-past, and that gave the good citizens of Auckland a head start to catch their trams or ferries in safety, before the boozers hit the streets. After work, a man with a thirst would have to race the clock to slurp down a few rounds of beer. Drinking was segregated so he could keep his mind on the task;

then everyone would spill out of the pubs after six and laugh, yell, fight or vomit in the streets, supervised by enormous numbers of uniformed police.

Six o'clock closing seems to me now to sum up neatly just about everything that was wrong about the 1950s – the oppressive regimentation, the pompous hypocrisy, the moronic timorousness, the contemptuous notion that Queen Victoria knew best – but at least, I suppose, the few of us who cared had a pretty clear notion of what we were kicking against. The targets for our humour, anger and occasional despair were monstrous in their self-righteous platitudinous grandeur, and easily identified.

In a way, of course, those who used Somervell's coffee bar as the centre of their social lives became as set in a uniform style of rejection and opposition as the 'respectable' dress and behaviour of the conformists they despised. The big difference, as I remember it, was that we got real coffee, while the rest of the population was still on what was euphemistically called coffee essence – a frightful concoction made from an extract of chicory. There was at least one decisive advantage in being a rebel.

37: FLIES ON A WALL

All the time, while I was hurling myself into Somervell's bohemianism and university politics, and beginning to jot rotten poems on the backs of envelopes, bills and lecture notes, I kept alive an entirely separate and equally devoted commitment to the outdoors. I joined the University Tramping Club, but tagged along just as regularly with the Auckland Tramping Club, which my father had belonged to more than thirty years earlier.

A good half of the weekends of the year saw me out in the hills around Auckland and the Coromandel, or at one of the huts on Mt Ruapehu, and I did several big trips to the Southern Alps – one of them as a passenger on the down train that was the last to cross the bridge at Tangiwai before it was destroyed by a lahar and the

Wellington–Auckland express was swept down the Whangaehu River with the loss of one hundred and fifty-one lives.

My companion on just about all these jaunts was a dedicated tramper and fine solo climber called Colin Hill, and I can claim to have had an unfortunate influence on his decision to go it alone on the big peaks.

Colin and I had been practising our snow and ice techniques on Mt Ruapehu for some months and we decided we were ready for the mountain's best climb: straight up the Pinnacle Ridge from the skifield below, followed by whatever traverse was necessary, then down the other side. There were no books we could find to help us, but we had studied the ridge from all angles and worked out a good steep climb with plenty of interesting problems. Because we were carrying heavy packs we decided we would free-climb on the ice without ropes. We couldn't afford crampons, so we agreed tolo take turns at cutting steps with our ice-axes.

It turned out to be a far more formidable test than we had anticipated and it took us a lot longer than we had allowed ourselves. Just short of the top I took the lead and put on a bit of speed, which meant that I skimped a bit on the steps. Colin slipped, but managed to fall on his axe, as we had practised often enough. It was a very nasty spot and there was no way, with the extra weight of his pack, that he could kick in his feet and give himself leverage to stand upright again. It was far too steep and we really should have been wearing crampons. Every time he tried to raise himself, the axe would rip through the ice like butter and he would slip a little further down.

I was okay. There was now only a short easy stroll to the top, whereas the way back to Colin seemed almost vertical. I sat on a rock outcrop and gave him some advice, which he was very pleasant about, considering the fix he was in. But there was nothing else for it, so eventually I had to secure my pack to a rock, which flaked alarmingly, sending bits free-falling through the air for hundreds of feet before landing. Then I managed to descend below him and cut a very big ledge that he could slide into safely. The one balls-up on what should have been a perfect climb was my fault entirely. I'd been in too much of a hurry and I felt angry with myself – and with Colin for not telling me to slow down and cut safe steps, though I couldn't very well tell him that at the time.

I didn't feel much better when we went some way along the ridge and found a nice slope to descend, only to face an overhang and a sheer drop down rotten rock before we could get to it. And the question was:

if we fell would it be onto snow or ice? If it was the latter we'd probably do ourselves an injury, not to mention take a fast ride over some huge bluffs that edged the slope. Colin was all in after his experience, and needed rest and a cup of hot tea, but I argued that if we stopped now and made a brew we'd have to bivvy up there for the night and the weather might close in on us. The sun was going down, so I said, 'Bugger it all, Colin. That white stuff down below us looks like snow to me,' and I threw my pack over the side, knowing that although it was a pretty safe bet, it was still about the most reckless thing anyone could do. But I wasn't going to try to hang on to a rock a couple of thousand feet up, with a friend who was understandably just about ready to curl up in his sleeping bag and try to get his nerve back.

Of course, my pack made a resounding plop. It was snow all right. And in a flash I was over the side too, without bothering to try climbing down the rock face. It was a wonderful sensation flying through the air and landing with a great squelch right up to my neck in gorgeous feathery snow.

We had a marvellous long glissade down the slope, steering ourselves with our ice-axes. But we were too late to find the hut we were aiming for, and had to sleep out in the tussock. We did a bit more climbing the next day then headed back to base. It was only then that we were interested enough to pore back through the log book at the Auckland Tramping Club hut and discover that no one had attempted our climb for two or three years. The previous traverse had been accomplished by a party that included two climbers called Edmund Hillary and George Lowe.

A couple of days afterwards we hitched a lift from two women, who drove us from the Chateau to National Park railway station. While we were chatting they asked if we'd watched the two climbers on the Pinnacle Ridge three days previously. Colin and I looked at each other. No, we said, almost simultaneously, we hadn't heard about that.

'Oh,' the driver said. 'It was the highlight of our holiday. Everybody at the Chateau was watching with telescopes and binoculars. It was terribly exciting. They were like flies on a wall. Some people were saying it was impossible and they'd never make it.'

'What? The Pinnacle Ridge?' Colin said. 'It's an optical illusion. That's the softest climb on the mountain.'

'It looked very difficult from where we were,' the other woman insisted. 'They seemed to be hanging on by their fingernails.'

'And they appeared to get in difficulties at the top,' the driver added.

'Just showing off,' Colin said with a laugh. 'The Chateau pays them to do it. It's to entertain the guests on sunny days.'

But it took another six months before Colin and I could really talk about the climb. We had met for a drink and Colin was trying to persuade me to attempt some South Island peaks. I said straight away that I was glad he'd asked me because I had something on my mind I'd like to tell him. The fact was that I would never go climbing again, with him or anyone else, because I hadn't liked what I'd seen inside myself when I'd had to go back and help him. It had taken a hell of a long time to skirt around below him and cut the big ledge for him to slide into. But there'd been no heroics or sense of duty. All I knew was that I was furious with myself for being such a bloody idiot to suddenly force the pace so near the top – and I'd been mad at him too for not shouting out to me to slow down and make a proper job of the steps.

Well, he said, he was bloody glad that I'd got hot under the collar, because if I'd kept my cool I may have worked out that it was too risky. Then he told me that he'd been bottling up the truth, too, and if I'd really like to know, he'd nearly shat himself all the time he was hanging there in case I woke up and used my common savvy and decided not to make it a double fatality. Then he added, 'But you're a bloody poet, aren't you? Which means you can always be relied on to act the maggot. I kept on reminding myself of that and it made me feel a whole lot better.'

Colin then confessed that he'd only asked me to come climbing again as a matter of form. From now on he had made up his mind that he was only going to climb solo. People would think it was crazy, but he didn't like what he had seen inside himself either.

I owed Colin a poem for that, but it didn't get written till a few years ago, when his wife rang up to tell me that he had come inside one day at home to rest on a chair, then had just slumped over, dead. It seemed such an odd and unlikely ending when I recalled that brilliant day and his great feats on mountains all over the country:

> The last rock at the top that for a time
> caps the rocks below is where we stand,
> also for a time. The summit of the ridge.
>
> Pebble, boulder and stone slab arrange
> a precedence. A backbone and a skull.
> Sooner or later, wind-worn, flaked by ice,

or kicked to bits by a boot, the line alters.
The next rock along becomes the new summit.
We search for the safe way down. The fall

comes years later, in a bed or an armchair,
a seat in a café, a patch of shade on the lawn
where you lean your back against a tree.

The view across the peaks always ends
at the wall of the sky, a bedroom door,
a prospect across a street and no farther,

a garden hedge. Calcium, phosphorus –
a ridge of minerals rising to a bone summit
where the eyes squint for the least perilous

descent, an outlook across a valley rattling
with pebbles and boulders. Your death rearranges
the view. Sitting safely beyond that place,

that time, suddenly you are flung into the sky.
I remember you as the shape of an eyelash.
A curved shadow of stone dislodged on the climb.

38: BOLTHOLES

Since I wasn't interested in completing my degree, the problem was to find a job where I could get through the day without exhaustion or heavy responsibilities, so I could get on with my reading – and writing the occasional poem.

It was my father who set the problem starkly. He pointed out that it was all very well rejecting academic ambitions and not becoming a schoolteacher at the very least, but there was no escape from paying the rent and the grocery bills – or, at least, there wasn't one that wouldn't in the long run be self-defeating, because a total evasion of all responsibilities would need such commitment and ceaseless ingenuity that it would eat up all my energies. That's what always happened to Bohemians, beachcombers and vagabonds. There were no half-pie solutions.

The irony was that a rejection of convention requires active and risky alternatives, which turn into just another kind of fulltime occupation. You get sucked into a system one way or the other.

So – according to my father – the proper question to ask was: Who was going to provide me with a sufficient financial return to be able to pay the bills, and at the same time provide a totally undemanding, non-exhausting working environment which wouldn't come with a secret package of take-home obligations and worries? And – he continued – if I thought about the proposition in those terms, I'd have to admit that what I was looking for wasn't so much an employer as a charity.

Of course I had to agree that he was about right. But I argued, perhaps a little weakly, that 'charity' wasn't the correct word. I wasn't on the bludge, I was looking about for something quite traditional and straight up and down. What I really wanted was a kind of literary bolthole. There had to be one somewhere.

It so happened that there *were* boltholes. They existed around magazines and newspapers, in Dickensian machine rooms, in reading rooms and at subediting desks – before new technology arrived and the power of the medieval guilds (which had transformed themselves – though in name only – into trade unions) was broken at last by the press magnates. But I didn't discover this for some time. The first stop I made in my quest was a classic mistake, but one that was easy to make: I chose the civil service.

Here was a setup that offered what was everywhere referred to as a cast-iron future. When I joined, people would slap my back and tell me that I was a lucky bastard. I had a job for life. Work began at eight in the morning. You signed the staff book as you walked in, making sure that you weren't consistently late, for a red line was drawn across the page at precisely 8.15 and you attracted unwelcome attention and your pay was docked if your name appeared regularly below it. Then at 4.30 you left the premises without a care in the world.

Admittedly it wasn't well paid, especially in the lower salary grades, but there were reliable annual increments in salary, and the work was partly useful, if you took a benign view of the welfare state – as most people right across the political divide did at the time. But the trouble was that it wasn't a soft job, and the place was full of able dedicated professionals.

I was astonished by this, for it didn't fit the popular picture of the typical pen-pushing, regulation-obsessed bureaucrat – and it was the factor that made the job intolerable. There was no escaping my colleagues' interest in my future. Courses, exams and promotion beyond my capacities and ambitions were set to snare me. And there were also the terrible dangers of the typing pool, a room full of stunning, nubile women, all on the lookout for husbands.

I remember a beautiful young typist sitting beside me one day, checking the text of a letter, when suddenly she leant close and dropped her hand on my thigh. I nearly passed out with the daring and the pleasure of the act. I thought: Wow, this is all right. But she lifted her hand away quickly, as though I wasn't supposed to read too much into what could easily have been no more than a temporary weakness of the wrist, and she said huskily: 'Have you ever been engaged?'

I gulped and told her no, I hadn't. She then whispered: 'Why not?' I told her the truth: I was far too young.

She looked at me in surprise. 'Friends of mine got married straight from school,' she announced. 'They weren't too young.'

Then she added, 'I'm not too young, am I?'

This was early 1950s New Zealand. The nation was a huge baby farm. State houses were being built by the thousands, the government paid a weekly cash bonus for every child under sixteen, there were subsidies on staple items of food, State Advances could supply young married couples with a cheap mortgage. I looked at the young woman and thought: If I stick around here I'm going to be filleted and hung out to dry in the breeze. The civil service was no place for me. There was nothing to be done but to scram, double-quick.

There was only one great benefit I got from the experience – the lifelong friendship I formed with the amazing John Kasmin. He and I met at a civil service conference where everyone had to make a speech, and since we were the only ones who considered we ought to take this opportunity to speak our minds, we sought each other out afterwards. Immediately we discovered we had books in common. That was enough. Within a week we decided to rent a bedsitter together in Mt Eden so that we could devote ourselves to books and bohemianism (which meant Somervell's coffee bar, the Golden Dragon restaurant and Bob Lowry and Odo Strewe parties, even though Kasmin didn't drink at the time).

Our friendship was highminded to a marvellous degree of absurdity. We would climb from our beds in the morning while it was still dark and sit naked on the verandah outside our window so that the first rays of dawn would strike our bodies and fill us with enlightenment. We would also go for long walks through the parks, embracing and kissing favourite trees so that the life-force that welled through them from the core of the earth would enter our chests and mouths and limbs. Actually, I could only last the distance on this kind of thing for about a week before I had to give up in embarrassment, but Kasmin had a genuine feeling for mysticism and hermetic religion, and manages to this day to keep an amused and watchful pineal body focused on them.

Later, in our separate post-civil service wanderings around the country, we met again in Wellington and shared another bedsitter, in Oriental Bay. Our interests had broadened considerably by then, and Kasmin had managed temporarily to include alcohol in his enthusiastic private studies and pursuits, so there was less highmindedness and a good deal more chaos in our daily lives. But there was still a lot of boisterous boyishness as well. In mid 1950s New Zealand, male adolescence could last almost till middle age. Alongside the sporty, beery mateship that represented the popular ideal of Kiwi manhood, and which most New Zealand men tried in some way or another to project in dress, speech and mannerism, there was nearly always the ghostly shadow of an immature and uncertain small boy. Sometimes this shadow gained substance in aggression and destructive violence, but often enough it transformed itself into clumsy yet harmless – and occasionally radiant – anarchy.

Years later I wrote Kasmin a poem about Oriental Bay which tried to capture a sense of the sheer fun of the life we shared, and the gauche boyishness of it all, and the way it also seemed so full of moments of magical illumination. It ended:

> in those days
> each morning
> rose like a firebird
> over the fume and ash
> of the town
> and snatched away
> the fowlyard gloom
>
> and in our place
> perched high above the bay
> we fought with pillows
> rolling hooting
> catching at small feathers
> which swirled in shafts of sun
> like tips of flame

39: Esmonde Road

At the end of the 1950s I remember sitting around with some friends and adding up how many jobs we'd had. It took some working out and we all lost count. The approximate figure I arrived at now escapes me, but I recollect that it was in excess of fifty.

It was a time of full employment and I worked here and there, sometimes for a few days only, all around both islands. If I got sick of a job, or felt like taking time off to go tramping or sit about and read, I just jacked it in. Work was something I had to do to gain leisure for books and other pleasures.

Many is the time I would wake up in the morning, feel an itch to be moving on, and decide to catch the Limited Express or hit the road and hitchhike to another town. Wellington and Auckland were interchangeable addresses. I don't remember how many dozens of times I moved between the two.

The only steady jobs I had after the year or so I spent in the civil service, were for two periods in the old Whitcombe and Tombs bookshops in Wellington and Auckland (when they really were shops for books); and at the end of the decade I also managed to stay put for almost a year, to save some money for travel, as a guide and general rouseabout at Waitomo Caves. In those days you didn't have special training or a uniform to be a cave guide, you just looked and listened to what was going on, then you took people underground and gave them a bit of misinformation about caves and glowworms, and tried not to get them lost or drowned.

It was only when I read Jack Kerouac's marvellous Whitmanesque hymn to life, *On the Road*, when it first appeared in 1957, that I realised that what we in New Zealand had called bohemianism was very similar to the attitude to life and the general behaviour that was now being referred to as 'beat' culture.

Being 'beat' meant freedom of spirit, freedom of employment and freedom of the roads. It was an entirely Pacific thing, which seemed to occur spontaneously and coincidentally in California, Australia and New Zealand. There was nothing like it in England or Europe till nearly a decade afterwards, and by then it had become ritualised and institutionalised into something better defined as 'hippie' culture. This tended to be less spontaneous and fluid as a movement, rather more self-consciously and politically 'alternative', and it was rigidly group or commune-structured. The two were definitely not the same thing. Being a hippie meant wearing a standard hairstyle and uniform dress, speaking a slack argot and behaving to a set of strict contra-rules. It may have been fun for a while, so far as the dope and sex went, but it was regimented and stultifying, and produced nothing of value except a few feeble tunes. It was only ever a time-out for conformists.

The ancestors of our peculiarly Pacific Bohemian-beat culture were people of the older generation, such as my grandfather, Mac – who had been brought up in hardships that never destroyed the wild and absurd pleasures and torments of their dreams – and the generation who followed them: people such as Denis Glover, A.R.D. Fairburn, Robin Hyde, Jean Devanny, R.A.K. Mason and Frank Sargeson – all of whom became writers. That they never became 'beat' (in the later sense of the word) was due partly to education, social background and upbringing, but mainly to their restricted mobility. They simply didn't have unlimited access to the roads.

It was my extraordinary good luck one night to call on Frank Sargeson. Kasmin had left our Mt Eden bedsitter for adventures in Wellington and the South Island, and I had returned home to Takapuna for a few months while I decided what I was going to do next. This meant that Frank was a neighbour again, and one evening Maurice Shadbolt came over to see me and asked if I'd ever dropped in on the man. When I said no, Maurice said, Well let's go and knock on his door.

Maurice and I have vastly different memories of who was there and what was said, but since several of his recollections of me, in his memoir *One of Ben's*, are entirely mistaken, however entertaining, I trust mine absolutely. Anyway, the outcome was that Frank invited me back to his little cottage at 14 Esmonde Road, and this led to a personal and literary friendship that would change my life.

For some months I got into the habit of calling several evenings a week. We would talk books and literary gossip, and I would always carry away an armful of reading matter to fuel future conversations. Janet Frame was living in the old army hut that was just outside the back door (in fact, the only door before Frank eventually built a small extension to the cottage and put in another entrance), and most evenings someone else would drop in to chat, swap books, drink tea or open the odd bottle of Lemora citrus wine. The legion that turned up on Frank's doorstep was as endless as its demands on his time and generosity were limitless, yet Frank gave from the wells of his spirit without reserve. It was as though he was a king of infinite treasure and no one who asked was ever denied.

That tiny fibrolite dwelling, set in the subsistence garden that Frank cultivated like a small farm, became a literary kingdom entirely without guards or frontiers and where the only cards of identity were books. As the novelist Dave Ballantyne put it: 'Here he wrote all his best-known short stories and novels, grew vegetables and entertained friends and fellow-writers. Here a truly New Zealand literature was born.'

When Janet Frame went to England, Frank took a few weeks' rest then said to me that over time quite a few people had confessed that what they had come to him for was to find his literary 'secret' – as if there was any such thing. The fact of the matter was that, although there really were such useful things as constructive advice and helpful criticism, there was no mystery, no hidden code, no magic formula that one writer could pass on to another. In other words, there was no secret and never would be. It was largely just hard work. A lot of people had a vague ambition to write, but it seldom came to anything because the only way to accomplish that ambition was to sit down and get on with the actual job of writing.

Therefore, he added, if I wanted to know how it was done, I'd better follow Janet into the army hut (Maurice Duggan was another 'graduate') and go through a pressure-cooker course in sitting down day in and day out at a desk with just an exercise book and a pencil, a typewriter and a ream of quarto paper, and getting through a set quota of work, the same as any other trade or calling.

Which is what I did. I began to learn to write work that was fit to publish – work which entitled me to think of myself, for the first time, not as someone who just happened to have a poem in his pocket, but as a real writer.

But the short move from our fine house in Rewhiti Avenue, across Lake Road to the army hut in Esmonde Road had its amusing side. When I told my father that I was going to Frank's place for a while, he was acutely embarrassed, then finally he took me aside and told me that there was something I ought to know. So far as he was concerned 'old Frank' may be a decent enough sort of chap, but there were rumours I probably hadn't heard that that he was one of the 'brown hatters'.

'Oh, you mean homosexual,' I said. 'Yes. Everyone knows that. But he's perfectly okay. He's a gerontophile.'

'What's that?' my father asked.

'Only attracted to older men – like you, I suppose,' I told him.

When I came to describe those marvellous times, in a poem I called 'A New Alphabet', the central lines went:

Standing behind the wooden bar

that marked the kitchen's frontier
and served as table, workbench,
secular pulpit, refuge,
he would hack peppers, wrench

lettuces apart, put tomatoes
to the knife, and feed the multitude.
A lectern where books were read from,
the place where tea was brewed,

a trading-post for counter-
intelligence, puns, wit, bile,
literary gas, good fun, outrage,
news from the street, guile,

interpretations of trifles,
wisdom. Everyone took
something of immeasurable value
away . . .

And, yes, that was it. Everyone came away with something to think about. I still turn up to Sargeson Trust meetings and functions at the old cottage, and each time I walk in it is in anticipation of mischief, surprises and the pleasure of good company.

40: What's in a name?

It was during a visit to Frank Sargeson's that, to my own surprise, I announced that since I was now beginning to think of myself as a 'real' writer, I was going to have a 'real' name, one that I had selected for myself.

'You'd better hurry up about it, then,' was Frank's only advice, 'because you've already started to publish and that's soon going to cause everyone a lot of confusion.'

He wasn't interested in the reasons for my decision, any more than – I was to discover decades later – he was interested in explaining how or why he had suddenly emerged as Frank Sargeson from the chrysalis of a boy who had been christened Norris Davey.

I think my father (who was hurt and offended) blamed Frank, as well as other friends, for my decision to adopt a name of my own, but all I can now remember is that it was my idea alone, and I cannot re-enter the ghost of the young man I then was to produce reliable and precise motives, if there were any.

So far as I can picture myself in relation to the world around me, I see two main drives in life from about the age of twenty: to get on a boat and leave the country for adventures overseas that would somehow enlarge my store of literary experience (and my encounters with alluring young women), and to change my name and become my own existential creation. That probably puts it rather more grandly than I would have at the time, but I think it captures the general idea.

There is a long tradition in New Zealand writing for choosing a name to live and publish by: Frank Sargeson, Katherine Mansfield, Robin Hyde, Renée and I are only a few such; for we must also take into account the long rollcall of women who have chosen (and still choose) to write under a name acquired from a marriage certificate. The problem in my case was that, unlike my friend Kasmin, who had put in a great deal of thought to invent that name – one which he would eventually make famous throughout the world of art – I found it easy to decide on the principle of starting off anew, but simply didn't have a clue what to call myself.

I was staying at the time with Odo Strewe and his family, in the new house they had moved to on the Scenic Drive at Titirangi, and one day Odo made me get off my arse and ring up a lawyer to draw up a deed poll, as I had said I wanted to, instead of dithering about with a pseudonym.

That was all very well, but as I left that day to keep the appointment with Frank Haigh, I still had no idea who exactly would be signing his name at the bottom of my poems. I thought of colours: Brown, Black, Green – but they were pretty used up. Then I considered occupations – but I was damned if I wanted to be another Butcher or Baker.

Finally, I got off the bus, since I had plenty of time to spare, and walked into town down Ireland Street. I was almost at the foot of the hill when I remembered seeing that same name somewhere else along the journey – on a hoarding or a building in New Lynn, I think, though I don't know exactly where – but that was good enough for me. I accepted the coincidence and that I'd been renamed by a street sign. I kept my appointment with the lawyer, paid my ten-shilling fee, and came out my own man.

Of course, I've occasionally had to wonder since how things would have turned out if I'd looked up and found the sign read Ladies Mile or Sea Horse Place.

Names haunt all of us. I have only to hear the sound we attach by custom to a person or place, for a torrent of memories to sweep through my mind. There are places, like the Haast Pass, which I tramped with the painter Mike Illingworth before the road was opened. Or Grafton Gully, where on a summer's night in 1958 I made love with my girlfriend beside the tombstone of one of the first settlers. Or Simla hut, in the Waitakere Ranges, which I shall always associate with weekends of talk and chess and bush-crashing with Colin Hill and Carl Freeman. Or The Terrace, in Wellington, where Maurice and Gill Shadbolt lived in a tiny house, and where I also lived for a while in a flat for an amazing year of reading, writing and escapades. Or Tina Anso's house in New Lynn, where I sat down before a typewriter with Barry Crump and announced that we were about to commit his first story to paper, a story that subsequently was transformed into chapter eight of A Good Keen Man. Or Birkdale, which in the mid 1950s was still half pastoral and which shall always be for me the scene of the finest tomato farm in the world – the place where John Graham, Robin Dudding, Anthony Stones, Frank Sargeson and myself were going to set up a theatre and a bookshop, but which ended up as one of the final settings for the adventures of Michael Newhouse in Sargeson's novel Memoirs of a Peon.

And there are names, such as Rangitoto, the syllables of which I carried about like an echo in my head even when, in the long years of my exile overseas, I would be working late at night on a newspaper or lying in the shade of a linden tree with a glass of wine outside a village bar in some Balkan village so remote that perhaps no other New Zealander had ever visited it before me.

These are the names that I recite to myself to locate small territories of the heart where the flags of my memories are never lowered.

41 : MOTHBALLS & GASOLINE

In the last two or three years of Mac's life I used to call on him as regularly as possible – usually once or twice a week. He lived near the top of Mt Eden Road, in a downstairs flat, at the back of an old wooden shop owned by his nephew Ted Hundleby, who ran a tiny grocery shop a couple of doors away and was a Justice of the Peace as well as being the Chairman of the Auckland Central branch of the Labour Party.

Mac shared the place with another pensioner called Charlie, who had only one interest in life – racehorses – and one topic of conversation – the complete contents of *Best Bets*, the racing pages of the *Star*, the *Herald* and Saturday's night's *Eight O'Clock*, and the racing commentaries on the radio. Charlie knew everything there was to know about blood lines, soft going and left-handed tracks. Even Mac, who had almost lived in the saddle in his early life, had to acknowledge that he had never met a man who knew so much about the New Zealand racehorse.

Although Mac tried to get Charlie interested in politics, and especially the betrayal of the left by Peter Fraser, the Anglo-Saxon suppression of Celtic civilisation and the glorious dawn of Soviet Communism, Charlie would hear him out patiently and politely, without listening, then return the conversation to the form at Matamata or Wingatui.

Mac would never bet on a horse without taking a close look at it first, and one day he suggested that Charlie and he should take a tram out to the Ellerslie meeting. Charlie was stunned.

'What?' he said. 'Go out to Ellerslie? Among the horses? Christ, a man might get trampled to death.'

When I called to see Mac a couple of evenings afterwards, he told me the story, wiping the tears of laughter from his eyes. It turned out that New Zealand's leading racing expert had never been on a racetrack. Charlie had never even been on the back of a horse in his life and in fact the closest he'd ever been to racehorses was to look at their photographs in the papers. 'The bugger doesn't even know which end the grass goes in,' Mac spluttered.

It didn't stop my grandfather from liking the man with a deep affection, for Charlie was impressive in his absurdity; and Mac died doing the man a service.

As Charlie told me at the funeral, 'Old Mac was the toughest bastard

I ever met,' he said. 'He had just made me a cup of tea when he started shaking violently. "Grab hold of this, boy, quick," he shouted at me. I didn't know what the hell was going on, but he just stood there shaking, and the cup was rattling like mad, so I took it. Then your grandfather fell down dead as a doornail in front of me and never spilt a drop.'

Mac's death seemed to me at the time to mark a point in my growing up when I could draw a line across all the events of my life and say I was making a new start.

I was nineteen. And the way I was told of the death was almost as surprising as the shock of the message itself.

A phone call came through to me at work and the news was broken to me by a woman whose voice I did not recognise. She explained that she was my mother. I hadn't heard her voice in nearly a decade.

She said that she would be going to the funeral and added that she hoped that wouldn't put me off attending. I told her it wouldn't, but it certainly meant that my brother and sisters wouldn't be there. The truth was that when Mac had come back to look us up after my mother and father's divorce, he – like my mother's lawyer – apologised to my father for supporting her side of the story. Mac often told all of us that he had come to realise that he had spawned a she-devil.

But I didn't go into all that. I listened while she went on to say that Percy Kelly and I would lead the pallbearers and Mac would be buried beside his wife in Hillsborough cemetery.

'A Christian burial?' I asked.

Yes, she said; her mother – Mac's wife – would have wanted a religious ceremony before Mac joined her in the grave.

'But she was a devout Catholic,' I said. 'And Mac was an atheist. How are you going to get around that?'

'We'll compromise with an Anglican service,' my mother said. It took me some time before I could see the funny side of that statement, but it struck me straight off that the woman I could remember debating with Jesuits had obviously changed in the decade-long gap since I'd seen her last.

This was only the first of many startling alterations. My mother had returned to teaching and had at last found an outlet for her enormous energies and talents, besides becoming one of the highest-graded teachers in the country. In a year or two she would become headmaster (there were only three women in the whole country at the time who became head*masters*) of one of Auckland's largest schools and make a great job of it. She had married again, happily, to a giant Scots ex-professional soldier called Jock Ward, and she had had another child, my half-sister Marion.

But I wasn't so interested in all that as in her appearance. The woman I now saw didn't look the slightest bit like the mother I'd known. I had preserved her memory for all those years as an attractive and dynamic woman in her thirties, who somehow combined three roles as a blue-stocking, a housewife and a mother who could walk out on her four young children. Now here she was, a highly successful middle-aged career woman and the contented matriarch of another family.

My mother offered me a drink after the funeral and I accepted it. The label on the bottle said it was sherry, but it didn't taste like that. Somehow the confusions of that day had affected my tastebuds. In a poem I wrote recently I said, 'It tasted of mothballs and gasoline', though I felt I had to add in the next line, 'Or perhaps I've imagined that.'

It's a taste and general impression that I sometimes can't get out of my mouth when I think about her. I've a fair idea it really has nothing to do with the drink. It's the flavour of a whole set of memories. Stale but still flammable.

42: FUNNY BUSINESS

If I ever try to recapture the flavour of those half-beat half-Bohemian days, I have only to think of the nights that I talked with friends till dawn at parties over a few cases of beer or an assortment of half-gallons of wine – or possibly just strong tea. Drugs, apart from alcohol or nicotine, didn't come into it.

Sometimes there would be meandering conversations that never got anywhere, but often enough there would be ferocious arguments about books, people and politics. I'm surprised, when I look back, to think that people such as Maurice Shadbolt or myself ever got any writing done, for we often talked ourselves to a standstill. The only person who never did was the poet James K. Baxter, who was as inexhaustible as he was hypnotically incoherent.

But nothing brings back the talk and the curious flavour of those days quite like the conversation I once had with a young woman called Christine, whom I saw only that one time and never heard of again.

There had been a party at the Lowrys', with endless joking and disputation, and somehow Christine and I ended up together. It turned out that she was a writer, though as far as I knew she had never published anything and in any case it soon transpired that her main ambition was to travel to Australia and become a folk singer. Since I had had a few poems printed here and there I thought this gave me an edge over her, but she turned out to be much sharper and smarter than I was.

She took me to her place in Princes Street, near the University, and the first thing she said as we stood outside the building was, 'Damn, I've forgotten my key.'

I told her to check her pockets again, which she did, though without luck. 'Okay,' she said. 'We'll just have to get in through a window. Give us a hand, will you . . .'

It didn't strike me as odd that she listened carefully outside several of the half-open ground-floor windows, because she explained that the tenants who lived behind them were real bastards who were always trying to get up her skirts and she didn't want to disturb them and start them off at this time of night.

Finally, she told me to shinny up a drainpipe to the second floor and work my way across to a window that was wide open and see if there was anyone inside, for she shared the room at weekends with another girl who just might be in there with a boyfriend. If there was any noise, she said, I should drop straight down again and we'd try around the other side of the building.

I climbed up. There was no sound, but I thought someone may be inside breathing quietly and I didn't want to scare them, so I sat on the sill staring in.

After a while I could make out the unmistakable shape of a hallway. There was no bedroom there at all. I had to laugh quietly at that. Christine couldn't even remember her own place.

I leaned out from the window and said in a loud whisper that if she went around to the back door I'd come down and let her in.

Christine also had a bit of a giggle when I told her of her mistake, but then she did another strange thing. She led me back upstairs and along the corridor, trying every door.

'Just to see if the bastards are locked in safely,' she explained, still giggling.

Eventually a door opened and she took me in. 'This is it,' she said.

The interior wasn't at all what I expected. There were a couple of romance novels lying on a table, but no other evidence of an interest in writing. There were the usual table, chairs and wardrobe, plus a couple of cupboards and a bed. On some shelves were china and a few dented pots and a pile of neatly folded blankets, but there were no sheets or pillowcases. There was also no food, no litter and there were no shoes or clothes to be seen. The place looked deserted and it smelled close and dusty.

As if guessing what I was thinking, Christine told me to open the window and let some air in. Then she checked it and told me she'd sent me up the wrong drainpipe for there was one just outside the window. That seemed pretty reasonable to me, and she explained further that she'd had just had a clean-up and she'd stacked her belongings in boxes downstairs. Since it would be too noisy to fetch them at this time of night, the best thing to do would be to kick our clothes off and sleep under the blankets.

I thought that was a pretty good idea, so I chucked off my clothes and climbed into bed. With the light still on, Christine undressed slowly, folding her clothes neatly across the back of a chair as she removed each item. She was very beautiful.

Then she bolted the door, turned the light off and got in beside me.

'Okay,' she announced. 'These are the rules. There's no funny business. No snoring. And if you drop a stinker you can sleep on the floor.'

'But why did you ask me here?' I asked in amazement.

'Because you're a writer and I want you to write about me,' she said. 'And you'll just forget me if I let you have the funny business.'

I hadn't heard it called that before, but I wasn't going to be pedantic. I told her she couldn't be more wrong. Funny business was great for the memory. In fact there was nothing better than it for casting your remembrances back as far as they could go and beyond.

But she insisted that she had learned enough about the writing game already to be sure in her own mind that what she said was true. I would never get around to writing about her if she gave me the funny business.

I spent a very uncomfortable half hour of desperate argument, naked beneath some rough and hairy blankets, before I finally fell into an exasperated asleep.

Then suddenly there was a fierce banging on the door.

'Who's in there?' a very angry voice demanded. 'Come out you bastard or I'll murder you . . .'

It was early Sunday morning, perhaps only seven o'clock, and I could instantly see why Christine had folded her clothes so methodically. She was out of bed and into her clothes and out the window before I'd assembled my gear and pulled my shirt and trousers on.

I threw my shoes and socks through the window and followed Christine as quickly as I could, which was very fast indeed. I had no idea what was going on, but I certainly knew that if she went down the drainpipe there was no sense in my walking out through the door. The cries of rage and banging were getting louder and you could hear doors slamming along the upstairs corridor and other people joining in the commotion. I picked up my shoes and socks and ran, following Christine across Albert Park then up Wellesley Street and down towards Victoria Park.

I was out of breath. Finally I sat down under a tree and pulled on my footwear and straightened my clothes.

'That wasn't your place at all,' I said. 'We could have got pinched for breaking and entering.'

'We didn't break anything,' she replied breathlessly. 'Except the world record for the hundred yards dash.'

I looked at her and shook my head and complained about the stupid unnecessary trouble she could have got us into.

'It was necessary,' she said.

'Why?' I demanded.

'Because of the way you pushed your tongue into my ear,' she announced.

'What?' I said.

'You don't remember?'

'No. You said there wasn't going to be any funny business.'

'Don't say you did it in your sleep and you can't remember anything about it,' she said with a laugh.

I told her she must be imagining things for I would certainly have remembered a thing like that.

'It just goes to show I was right, doesn't it?' she said.

I demanded to know what she was getting at now.

'What I was telling you last night,' she said. 'About forgetting if . . . You know . . .'

'The funny business?' I asked.

'Well?' she demanded. 'Will you promise me? Have I done enough? Do I get a whole chapter to myself? In the book you'll write one day?'

'Yes,' I said. 'You've earned your chapter.'

And we both laughed and agreed to meet again that night, though she never turned up. I waited for her for a couple of hours then had to smile to myself, thinking that perhaps she was on the far side of town looking for another place to slip into and sleep for the night before going to Australia.

It's odd how right she was. It was a small event and it could easily have been overlaid by other memories in forty years of happenings that seemed far more significant at the time. But for me it captures the essence of the times uniquely – the unpredictability and the bizarre reasoning and convoluted arguments that kept us fired up – and she was just plain brilliant. Even if she never reads this, I'm certain that she knew she'd always be remembered. And I'm just as sure that she knew I'd keep my word.

43: A LIFE AFLOAT

I lent Bob Lowry the first fare I had raised to travel overseas, and afterwards told myself truthfully that the gesture wasn't really generosity on my part, for at the time Bob needed the money far more to stay in business in Auckland than I needed it to go off on a jaunt to London. I was also self-aware enough by then to know that I was practising a kind of evasion. I wasn't really ready to go anywhere. I still didn't have a good enough reason to satisfy myself.

But the second time I raised the fare, which was in 1959, when I'd been working for some time at Waitomo Caves, everything happened so quickly that I didn't have time to think about it, let alone question my excuses or intentions.

It all happened very conventionally. I met an Australian woman on holiday and within a few weeks we had gone to bed together and decided to get married and live happily ever after, which is the way things sometimes occur at the age of twenty-six, as well as at other times in your life – as I'd be the last person in the world to deny.

Anyway, she took off back to New South Wales to make the wedding arrangements, and somehow or other, by the time I crossed the Tasman, we'd decided we were being foolish and called it off – and that's also the way things sometimes happen when you're that age and even at other times of your life.

Which is how I came to stay with my uncle Frank in Sydney until I had a gutsful of him, and until, as I was walking down a street one day in 1959, I saw these almost give-away fares on an old immigrant ship called the *Toscana*, which was making its last voyage in only a few days' time, back to Venice, then to the breakers.

I was living in Kings Cross, in the first entirely bookless house I had ever seen in my life – there wasn't even a comic or a copy of the *Reader's Digest* in it – and I had just enough money for the fare with about ten bob over to keep me going across the Continent and into England, so I paid up on impulse and thought I'd just have to tighten my belt till the ship left. I was feeling very hungry indeed when I had the miraculous good luck to bump into my old school friend Alan McNeish, walking down a Sydney street. Alan was working for the Australian Broadcasting Corporation. He had a good laugh at my plight and fed me a couple of marvellous meals that sustained me, and he even came down to the wharf and waved me goodbye.

And so a whole new life began. At Melbourne, which was the next port we called into, an eccentric-looking man with very long hair and a beautiful blonde wife joined the one hundred and eighty-odd passengers, and it was only a couple of years ago, when reading Barry Humphreys' memoir *More Please*, with its account of travelling on the same ship, that I realised who my fellow passengers must have been. I never once spoke to the Humphreys, though the voyage was one long wallow, with stops at Perth, Colombo, Aden, Suez and an alarmingly perilous village harbour on the east coast of Greece, besides a mechanical breakdown in the Red Sea. I thought I had already left the Antipodes in my mind and didn't want to meet anyone who may have turned my thoughts homewards. The only passengers I spoke to were the small group with whom I shared a cabin and a table.

I can remember them now. There was a crazily entertaining Frenchman whose brilliant conversations were manufactured out of nothing, for he couldn't speak English any more than I could speak

French (though that didn't stop either of us); two reserved and fastidious Dutchmen who, without a word about the favour they were doing us, always slipped their carafes of red wine across the table to the Frenchman and myself – for wine was served to everyone free with lunch and dinner. There was also a sullen and profoundly obtuse Australian who had to be told after every meal to go and jump in the bloody drink – and it became my regular and expected duty to point out which exit he should go through to find it – and finally there was a dull, almost entirely taciturn German who got drunk one night and confessed in a surprising outpouring of words that he had served in the SS as a boy of seventeen, in the last months of the war, and deeply regretted doing so. The memory harrowed him, and I believed his pain.

Then there was the miracle of the ship's library. I was sure I could picture the person who had selected it, for it was one of the most extraordinary collections of modern fiction first editions I've ever come across anywhere. The fate of these books seemed uncertain, but it never crossed my mind to help myself to them. That would have been far too unlucky. And then there was . . .

But all that lies outside the design of this narrative, which has its beginning with birth – and it's ending in a farewell.

*   *   *

There remains just one small yet crucial event that I have to record. It took place not long before I left Auckland and it seems to me now to just about sum up and round off those first twenty-six years of my life. The time in which, for ever and for good or bad, I became a survivor and a writer.

I had already decided that I didn't want to go through the marriage with the Australian woman, but I knew I had to go over and face up to the situation I had at least half created; so I did what may not have been the best thing to do in the circumstances, but it was a gesture that seemed necessary at the time.

I rang a woman I knew in Auckland and asked if we could meet. The woman laughed and said if it was my forthcoming marriage in Australia that I wanted to see her about then forget it – I'd talked myself into it, so I could talk my way out again. But if I wanted to see her for her own sake then she'd meet me off the Devonport ferry and I could come out on a boat trip which she and some friends had organised off Stanley Bay that night.

It was a night of wonder. No one actually wanted to go anywhere in particular, so we turned the little outboard engine on every now and again, and in between just floated about, having a few drinks and joking and laughing a lot. There was a crate of quart bottles of beer on board and a bottle each of Brajkovich's Kumeu Red and Kumeu White – our first honest wine labels.

At one point we followed one of the narrow channels up Shoal Bay and stepped out onto mudflats and mangroves, leaving deep squelching tracks, and had to hang our feet over the gunwales later to clean the muck off.

Then we headed up harbour and passed near the caissons for the piers of the new harbour bridge. We slipped underneath part of the structure, then someone said it was getting late, so we went about and steered slowly back towards the mooring again.

As we did so, the moon came out from behind a cloud and lazily we rocked in the ruts of the track it left down the full length of the harbour.

I reached over and dangled my hand in the gold of the moon and thought how fortunate I was to have a friend like the woman beside me. It was then that she said to me, 'So, you're going to go through with it. You're really leaving in a few days, after all, aren't you?'

'Yes,' I agreed.

'Well,' she said. 'I've got a feeling that you'll be away much longer than you think. People always do. So I probably won't ever see you again, will I?'

I shrugged and didn't attempt an answer.

'But you'll always remember tonight, wherever you go,' she went on. 'And do you know why?'

'Because of you?' I asked, thinking that was what she wanted me to say.

She shook her head and we both sat in silence for a bit.

Then she said, 'Because tonight's the way it's always going to be for you. You've had a lot of confrontation already in your life, haven't you?'

I agreed that I had and admitted that quite a bit of it was of my own making.

'Well, you won't have to cross many bridges again, you'll float beneath them. And as for the moon, we've been gliding right over it for the past half hour.'

'Under the bridge and over the moon?' I asked.

'Most of the time, and with a bit of luck. Perhaps it's just a way of saying you'll always have poems in your pocket and stars in your eyes,' she said, and she laughed. And when her friends asked what was so funny, she explained and they too laughed.

Everyone was in a good mood that night. And she was right. I've managed to slip under most bridges and, often enough, float over the moon too, and to keep writing poems and hold on to my best illusions. That's what she was getting at. The life I would lead would be all about books and writing. And I have never forgotten a word she said.

But now it's not so much the words that matter. The woman is dead and mostly it has been the sound of her laughter I hear when I close my eyes.

Once that sound seemed golden and bell-like in my remembrance. But now it echoes a cry that becomes ever more distant, forlorn and full of nostalgia. It is the cry of a nightbird winging over the still waters as a cloud veils the moon and the tide is about to sweep in over the tracks we left across the mudflats and through the mangrove swamps, and obliterate all sign of our passing.